Leading the Living
Organization

Leading the Living Organization

Organization

GROWTH STRATEGIES FOR MANAGEMENT

Lane Tracy

QUORUM BOOKS

Westport, Connecticut • London

Copyright Acknowledgments

Portions of Chapters 1, 3, 5, 6, 7, 8, and 9 were originally published by the College of Economics, Nihon University, in Lane Tracy, "Design for Organizational Health," *Journal of Business Research*, no. 12 (1992). Reprinting of these portions is by permission of the Research Institute Administration Office, College of Economics, Nihon University, Tokyo, Japan.

Permission was granted by McGraw-Hill, Inc. to quote from James G. Miller, *Living Systems* (New York: McGraw-Hill, 1978). Specific citations are in the notes.

Library of Congress Cataloging-in-Publication Data

Tracy, Lane.
    Leading the living organization: growth strategies for management
/ Lane Tracy.
      p.   cm.
    Includes bibliographical references and index.
    ISBN 0–89930–819–8 (alk. paper)
    1. Management.   2. Organizational behavior.   3. Leadership.
  I. Title.
  HD31.T674   1994
  658.4′092—dc20   93–41817

British Library Cataloguing in Publication Data is available.

Library of Congress Catalog Card Number: 93–41817
ISBN: 0–89930–819–8

First published in 1994

Quorum Books, 88 Post Road West, Westport, CT 06881
An imprint of Greenwood Publishing Group, Inc.

Printed in the United States of America

The paper used in this book complies with the
Permanent Paper Standard issued by the National
Information Standards Organization (Z39.48–1984).

10 9 8 7 6 5 4 3 2 1

Contents

Figures and Tables

FIGURES

TABLES

Preface

We are all members of organizations. Most of us work for one. Many of us are volunteers for one or more. Many of us worship in organizations. Some of us manage them or even create them.

The basic thesis of this book is that these organizations are, or should be, alive. They are living systems and should be treated as such. They are living because they derive many of their most important characteristics from the genetic makeup of their members. Because of their origins, organizations exhibit the same essential processes and structures that you and I display.

Part of the task of this book is to explain just what those essential processes and structures are. But this only lays the foundation for a more important assignment. If organizations are living systems, they should be treated as such. The bulk of the book, therefore, is devoted to the question: How should a living organization be managed?

This is not a scientific question. It is a practical problem. The first step toward a solution is to learn to look at organizations as life forms. This perspective, when mastered, reveals a certain degree of natural wisdom in the way we traditionally structure and manage organizations. Yet it also exposes many flaws in our conventional management methods. The living systems perspective enables us to diagnose these errors and correct them. It also assists us in coping with change that may call for creative response, organizational mutations so to speak.

If you accept the basic premise that organizations are alive, you should find this book very helpful as a guide to managing them. The book is,

among other things, a manual on the care and feeding of living organizations. But it is also, of necessity, a polemic and a treatise. Because we are
not used to thinking of organizations as living systems, I must present
arguments to show that they really are alive and explicate the consequences of that fact. I hope you will bear with me if, at times, the argument becomes complex. We will always come back to practical matters.

Some of the conclusions and practical pointers will probably seem
obvious to you. That is because, in certain cases, living systems analysis
simply confirms the wisdom of current managerial practice. In such
cases, the book provides a firm theoretical basis for what we know from
experience. The real worth of the theory, however, is when it leads to
novel conclusions. I hope you will encounter at least a few "Ah-hah!"
reactions as you read.

At its core this book is intended to help you cope with your role as a
leader or member of a living organization. It will aid you in diagnosing
organizational illnesses and prescribing treatment. It may, if necessary,
enable you to resurrect a dead organization or start a new one.

Early in the book I will describe a couple of typical, young business
organizations. We will then follow their progress as we examine a variety
of issues that are illuminated by the living systems perspective. These
organizations are composites; any resemblance to real organizations, living or dead, is coincidental. Nevertheless, I hope you will be able to identify with the managers of these illustrative firms. Their travails are typical
of those faced by managers everywhere. They demonstrate the problems
of being the "head" of a living entity.

In writing the book I have tried to keep living systems jargon to a minimum. Yet some technical terms are essential. Whenever they are introduced, they are italicized and defined. There is also a glossary of these
technical terms at the back of the book.

Another feature of the book is that useful conclusions and practical
advice are highlighted. Either they are summarized in a special section at
the end of the chapter, or they are indented and italicized.

A careful reader will note a certain amount of repetition from one chapter to another. Please do not think that I am running out of material. The
cause of this repetition is the systems approach. Each chapter looks at the
whole organization, but from a different angle or perspective. Consequently, we see some of the same features each time, but slightly altered.
It is a bit like circling a transparent plastic model of the organization, seeing things differently from each side.

Many of the ideas in this book were pretested in a series of lectures at
Nihon University, Tokyo, Japan. I am indebted to Professor Seiji Muro-
moto and Assistant Professor Takashi Hiroi for inviting me to prepare
those lectures. In preparing the manuscript for the book I was aided by
my wife, Athena, who proofread it. Graphics were created by Lisa Slates

and Peggy Sattler of the Ohio University Learning Resources Center. Amy Van Horn helped me prepare the index. Eric Valentine of Quorum Books and anonymous reviewers provided tips on how to improve the product. I take responsibility for everything else.

Leading the Living
Organization

Chapter 1

Managing a Living Organization

Are organizations alive or dead? That is the first question raised by this book. How you go about managing an organization depends on your answer to this question.

How can we tell whether an organization is alive or not? Is there a heartbeat we can listen to? Are there brain waves we can scan? No, the telltale signs are not the same as for human life. But there are key indicators of life, depending on our position within the organization. Here are some questions to ask.

KEY QUESTIONS

If you are a founder or owner of the organization, must you frequently provide infusions of new capital, or does the organization generate sufficient income to meet its own needs? A living organization must be able to acquire sufficient resources to maintain a steady flow of material, energy, and information through the system.

If you are a leader of the organization, do you constantly have to give it new instructions? Or does the organization make decisions for itself in accordance with a few guiding policies and procedures? A living organization must be capable of making its own decisions.

If you are a manager in the organization, does it respond readily to changes in its environment? Or does it wait for you to point out what is happening and force you to jump start the reaction? A living organization monitors its environment and responds in such a way as to maintain equilibrium or to take advantage of opportunities for growth. Of course, as part of the organization you are expected to do your part of the monitoring and responding, but you shouldn't have to do it all.

If you are a member or employee, do you and your colleagues act for the good of the organization? Or do employees all seem to act in their own interests? The decisions and acts that are made in the name of a living organization must be guided by the organization's interests, however imperfectly those interests are understood.

Is the organization selective about inputs? Or can anyone become a member, regardless of qualifications? And does the organization accept goods and information without checking their quality? A living organization must have a boundary that protects it from harmful inputs.

If you are a client or customer of the organization, does it serve your needs well? Or is it often late, is the quality poor, is the price not right? A living organization serves other systems well in order to maintain a healthful relationship with its environment.

Few people find themselves in organizations that are truly dead. The people in a dead organization are quickly dispersed to unemployment lines, new jobs, or their homes, leaving only a skeleton of empty, unused buildings. But many people are members of dying organizations and many others work in puppetlike organizations that exist only as long as the founder wills them to.

The preceding indicators are only a few of the ways in which a healthy, independent organization can be distinguished from a dying or dependent one. Later we will uncover many additional signs of life. We will also be concerned with the health of the organization—it may be alive but ailing. Management, as we will see, is mostly a matter of maintaining the health of a living organization through proper diagnosis and treatment.

But first, how do organizations get to be alive or dead? This is determined primarily by the beliefs that the founder(s) and other key people have about the nature of organizations.

BELIEFS ABOUT THE NATURE OF ORGANIZATIONS

Organizations mean different things to different people. Founders and managers treat organizations in a variety of ways. Some founders and managers act as though the organization is an extension of themselves. The organization's success is their success; an attack on the organization is a personal attack on them. Such leaders tend to treat other members of the organization as part of the family.

A related view is that the organization is the founder's "baby." It is a separate living entity created in the founding parent's image. The parent hopes that the organization will thrive and carry the torch well beyond his or her lifetime. Managers, if they accept this view, treat the organization as a living institution that has been put in their care. They will usually encourage other members to take a similar view.

A quite different perspective is that the organization is a private possession of the founder or owner. It is a thing to be used for personal purposes or a trophy to be added to the collection. Other members are considered to be "hired hands," their time and loyalty purchased to do a specific job.

A somewhat similar view is that the organization is a tool, a means to an end. The end may be personal or it may be shared by the other members. In either case, it is an objective that the founder or manager could not accomplish alone. The task requires the cooperation of other people and the accumulation of capital. It may also dictate that the organization must become a legal entity, such as a corporation or partnership. The organization is a machine at the disposal of the leader, and the members are part of that machine. The members may be hired hands or they may be willing participants who share many of the goals of the organization.[1]

When founders and managers view the organization as a tool or a possession, it is born dead. The organization is like a puppet. The only life in it is the life force of the individual members willing the organization to perform its dance.

Living organizations originate from the belief that an organization has a life of its own, or at least that it is an extension of our own lives. The former belief leads to a truly independent entity serving its own purposes, the latter belief to a symbiotic system. Both are living organizations, but the first is *totipotential* (capable of carrying out all of the processes necessary to life)[2] and able to survive beyond the life span of its founders, whereas the second dies when its host dies.

Role of Founders and Managers

The view that founders and managers take of an organization determines how they see their own role. If the organization is simply a means to an end, they will look at it in terms of its efficiency and effectiveness. They will be concerned about devising good structures and processes and maintaining smooth operations. They will act like mechanics who are trying to keep the machine in good working order, at least until the end is accomplished.

If the organization is seen as a possession, the founder or manager's role will be to exploit it or increase its value. The organization has worth only so long as it adds value to its owner. It may be maintained and augmented, provided that it has continuing usefulness, or it may simply be squeezed dry and discarded.

Founders and managers who perceive the organization as a living entity, whether as an extension of themselves or as a separate creature, tend to view their role as being a parent, steward, or physician. As parents they attempt to guide and instruct the organization in right paths. As stewards they seek to preserve the organization and help it to attain its potential. As physicians they monitor the health of the organization, attempting to diagnose and treat its ills in order to maintain it in a healthy state.

This book adheres to the view that organizations are separate living entities. The role of the founder is, first, to provide a good *template* or charter for the organization. The template must provide a set of values as well as instructions for the establishment and growth of structures and processes that will enable the organization to thrive in its environment.[3] Second, the founder must provide nurturance in the early days of the organization, until it is able to stand alone and fend for itself.

Managers, from this perspective, are stewards and physicians. As integral parts of the organization, managers must make decisions based on organizational values and for the sake of the organization. They must also attend to the health of the organization, protecting it from predators and invaders, keeping it well fed with resources, leading it into favorable environments, modifying its behavior, diagnosing its illnesses, and prescribing appropriate treatments.

Managers and founders alike must understand that the organization has a life of its own, that it has a right to survive and develop its potential, and that it may well outlive them. It is not just a possession or a tool for their own ends. Their role, if they choose to accept it, is to make good decisions for the organization based on *its* values, purposes, and goals.

Viewpoint of this Book

If you accept the view that organizations are living systems, or even if you don't but are intrigued by it, I believe you will find this book interesting. It presents the logical consequences of this viewpoint, as they apply to such managerial topics as motivation, leadership, decision making, management of change, conflict resolution, stress, organizational structure, boundaries and protection, communication and information flow, corporate culture, efficiency and effectiveness, growth, and renewal.

The focus of the book is on practical matters. For example, if the organization is a living entity with its own values and motives, how does a manager go about "motivating" the organization? How do the manager's motives interact with those of the organization, and how does the organization motivate the manager? How can the manager deal with conflict between selfish motives and the need to serve the organization as a decision maker? Why is corporate culture such an important aspect of a mature organization, and what is the manager's role in shaping and maintaining that culture? How do organizations attempt to protect themselves from disease and predators, and what role do managers play in this process? As you can see, the living-organization viewpoint raises some practical questions that are not usually confronted in more traditional treatments.

Before we can launch into these practical matters, however, we should examine whether this viewpoint has merit. Is it reasonable to conceive of organizations as living entities? Do they have values and rights independent of the values and rights of their members? What are the characteristics of organizations that might cause us to accept their status as living systems? The remainder of this chapter is devoted to these questions and to a preview of the other chapters.

CHARACTERISTICS OF LIVING SYSTEMS

Think of an organization that is very familiar to you. It could be a business firm, a government bureau, a social or religious organization, or an institution of higher learning. Now imagine that organization as an animal or plant. What is the organization like? Is it a tiger, waiting to pounce on unwary competitors and other denizens of the "jungle out there"? Is it an elephant, patient and strong, with a long memory? Is it a rose, displaying beautiful blossoms protected by a fence of thorns? Is it a whale, swimming gracefully, spouting occasionally, and grazing among the small fish? Is it a weed, growing rapidly in many directions, choking out other life? Or is it a snail, plodding slowly but steadily toward its goal, never leaving its shell?[4]

However you may have pictured your organization, I suspect you had no difficulty imagining it as an animal or plant. Like animals and plants, organizations are living entities with specific characteristics. Each organization has its own "personality."

There are also "species" of organizations. Business firms differ in general and predictable ways from government bureaus, political parties, universities, and social organizations. Within each of these broad groups there are subclassifications. Manufacturing firms differ from retail, service, and financial firms. Large, multinational manufacturing firms differ from small, regional ones.

Like animals and plants, these varieties of organizations exist in a shared environment and compete among themselves for resources. They are born, they may grow and prosper, and eventually they die or are absorbed into another entity. There are many other ways in which organizations are similar to organisms. The basic reason for these similarities is that organizations, like animals and plants, are living systems. They exhibit the processes, structures, and subsystems that are necessary to life.

What is life? I think we would all agree that plants and animals personify life. Whatever the common defining characteristics of plants and animals may be, those are properties of life. For instance, plants and animals reproduce themselves by processes such as cloning, conception, or seed germination. Anything claiming to be alive must demonstrate a similar ability to reproduce. Plants and animals also act independently to maintain themselves in a changing environment; they receive inputs of matter, energy, and information, transform them, and expel outputs of altered matter, energy, and information; and they have a distinct boundary separating them from their nonliving environment.

Organs such as the human heart and kidneys show similar characteristics. Organs have well-defined boundaries, they process inputs and produce valuable outputs, and they maintain themselves so long as they remain attached to the host organism. Organs are not totipotential; they cannot reproduce by themselves, but are able to do so through the reproduction process of a host organism. Although symbiotic with organisms, organs can often be kept alive outside an organism for short periods while awaiting a transplant operation.

Even single cells are alive. Perhaps in biology lab you once peered at a paramecium through a microscope, watched it move and ingest something or divide and separate into two cells. It displayed all of the properties mentioned above: a boundary, reproduction, purposeful action.

But what about a group—a family, for instance, or a wolf pack or a grove of trees? Is a group alive? Does it have a boundary? Does it reproduce and display purposeful behavior? Does an organization—a business firm or a hive of bees, for instance—possess the characteristics of life? How about a community, such as your hometown; is it alive? Is the United States alive as a nation or society? What are the characteristics that cause us to say that something is alive?

Physical Characteristics

One of the properties shared by cells, organs, and organisms is that they are all composed primarily of protoplasm. Because of this composition they can exist only in an Earthlike environment. Gravity, temperature, air pressure, and radiation must be within a certain range; likewise, the percentages of oxygen and carbon dioxide in the air and the amount of water available must be capable of sustaining carbon-based life.

Yet, isn't this also true of *social systems*—that is, groups, organizations, communities, nations, and supranational systems (e.g., the United Nations)? The primary *components* of social systems are organisms. The basic stuff of which groups and organizations are made is the same as the protoplasmic substance of organisms. Ergo, human social systems are composed primarily of protoplasm and require the same environmental conditions as the people of which they are comprised.

Although people are the primary ingredients, human social systems also encompass other components. For instance, a business firm consists not only of individual employees but also of work groups, task forces, committees, departments, plants, and divisions. Each of these components may be a living system in its own right.

Another class of components is *artifacts*, which are nonliving parts of the system. In a business firm, these may consist of buildings, roads, fences, gates, vehicles, machinery, furniture, and inventory.

Templates

Cells, organs, and organisms also contain genes. Genes provide the template or program for maintenance of the existing structure and processes of the system, for growth and development of the system, and for reproduction.

The template is a central feature of life. After extensive study of both biological and social systems, James G. Miller found that every living system has a set of basic instructions from the beginning of its existence.[5] These instructions, the template or charter, govern the interaction of the component parts and subsystems, and provide a guide for the development of the system.

For cells, organs, and organisms, the basic template is supplied by genes composed of deoxyribonucleic acid (DNA) molecules. Genetic templates also provide part of the basis for social systems, developing organic structures and processes that underlie the formation of bee hives, schools of fish, and human families. But something more is needed. Dawkins pointed out that some ideas are like genes; the information they carry enables them to be replicated and spread throughout a population. Popular songs, fads and fashions, jokes, and slogans have this quality. Dawkins called such ideas *memes*.[6]

Certain memes have the further property of generating groups and organizations. For instance, the rules of a game perform a role in the formation of teams to play it. Shared ideas of entertainment may generate a social group, such as a sewing circle or book discussion group. The script for a play prompts a cast to be formed to perform it. A new business is organized in accordance with a corporate charter, a franchise agreement, or the entrepreneurial ideas of the founder. A set of religious beliefs generates a congregation or a group of monks. A political concept induces the formation of a political party, a movement, or a nation. Thus, social systems are governed in part by a template, which consists of memes such as rules, norms, a charter, contract, script, creed, manifesto, or constitution. This *memetic template* supplements the underlying set of instructions supplied by the genetic templates of the social system's members.

Maintenance

Another primary characteristic of life is that it is capable of sustaining itself. It does so by acting on the environment to obtain necessary resources, transforming them into useful products and energy, and expelling products and wastes. In systems terms, this means that all living things are *open systems*. It also means that these living systems act purposefully to maintain themselves against the ravages of entropy and environmental change. The basic character of the system is maintained even as new components are added and old ones are sloughed away.

Perhaps it is in this characteristic of preserving constancy through flow and change that the equivalency of all living systems is easiest to see. Nonliving open systems, such as automobiles and computers, acquire inputs, transform them, and extrude outputs. But they do not maintain themselves. An automobile does not repair its own valves or grow new tire tread to counteract wear. It does not seek gasoline and oil to replace that which has been consumed. Only by making the automobile an adjunct or component of a living system can it acquire this maintenance capability.

A business firm, on the other hand, does try to repair and maintain itself. It replaces or retrains personnel when necessary. It preserves, repairs, or replaces machinery. It seeks new inventory to restock what has been sold, and new orders to supplant those that have been completed. So long as the flow of resources is adequate to sustain the business, and leadership is present to provide purposeful direction, the organization can maintain itself indefinitely.

Groups, communities, and nations show a similar propensity for maintaining themselves. Groups seek to retain members, enforce norms of behavior, and defend their territory. Communities strive to retain industry to sustain the local economy; uphold law and order through police and courts; maintain an infrastructure of streets, sewers, and water mains; and preserve the history of the community in archives and libraries. Nations collect taxes to pay for upkeep of the infrastructure, protection of borders, education of citizens, conservation of the environment, and preservation of economic balance. At each level of social systems, maintenance of the existing system consumes much of the energy and attention of leaders and members.

Actualization

Although maintenance of steady states is essential, living systems do more than simply sustain themselves. They also seek to actualize their potential. That is, they grow and develop in accordance with instructions from their template.

Organs and organisms begin with a single cell that grows and divides in very specific fashion, developing into something that is capable of much more than the original cell. Through learning processes some organisms continue their development even beyond the programming supplied by their genes.

Social systems are more flexible in their growth, having the capability to reorganize themselves. If a business idea shows potential, a firm can actualize it by adding employees and machines, moving to new quarters, developing specialization and departmentalization, retraining employees, adding new levels of leadership, and so forth. The difficult trick for social systems is to maintain the essence of the original system amid all of this purposeful change.

Groups seek to grow by attracting new members, but also to maintain the group's current character by socializing the new members in the norms and traditions of the group. Organizations likewise provide orientation and training for new members and seek to blend new capital acquisitions into the existing structure, although some change may be necessary. Communities and societies employ education and the law to merge immigrants and new generations into the culture, but education is also used to help citizens adapt to technological and political change.

Tension between the requirements of maintenance and actualization is an essential feature of living systems. It is impossible to preserve the status quo completely and, at the same time, grow and develop. When the mandates of maintenance and actualization clash, a choice must be made. How the system makes this choice will be discussed in Chapter 3.

Propagation

Another familiar feature of biological systems is that they propagate. The most obvious form of propagation is sexual reproduction. Plants and animals create new systems with characteristics similar to themselves by transmitting and combining their templates through spores, seeds, eggs, sperm, and the like. The new, combined templates then generate systems that are near replicas of the originals. Indeed, parts of the new system, specific DNA sequences, are exact replicas.

Do social systems propagate as biological systems do? If we conceive of propagation strictly in terms of sexual reproduction, this does play a role in the propagation of families and societies. Each new generation of a family is a partial replica of the previous generation. When the European colonists came to the Americas, they created new societies in the image of the societies from which they had come, part of that image stemming from racial traits imparted by sexual reproduction.

Yet, we should not think of propagation only in terms of sexual reproduction. Even biological systems have other means of replicating themselves, such as cloning and cell division. Organs lack their own reproductive capacity, but use the reproductive facilities of their organismic hosts in order to propagate.

If propagation includes *any* means by which a living system can create new systems similar to itself, then social systems have found a variety of ways to do this. Some business firms have a franchising subsystem that creates new units in the mold of the original. Thus, we see a proliferation of fast-food restaurants that are like clones of the archetype. Other firms build new plants or create new divisions and eventually spin them off as independent units. Religious denominations found new congregations through missionary work. Professional sports leagues create new teams in the mold of the current members. Universities establish branch campuses that sometimes grow to become independent units. Fraternities, sororities, civic clubs, and secret societies "colonize" by chartering new units on campuses and in cities.

Note that social systems, and some organisms as well, may propagate both the memetic and the genetic parts of their templates, or either part separately. Propagation of plants and lower animals is basically genetic, but humans and other primates seek to transmit family norms of behavior, as well as their genes, to their offspring. Authors, composers, and artists seek immortality through dissemination of their visions and ideas. Business firms often attempt to spread their special products, services, or way of doing things, as when Apple patents its particular computer architecture and tries to gain adherents to it.

Political parties are primarily involved in memetic propagation; that is, with ideas about how the government should operate. But religious groups and societies may disperse their unique characteristics through both intermarriage and education-socialization processes. For instance, most Christian churches attempt to indoctrinate the children of members through Sunday school and rituals such as baptism and confirmation.

Universities seek to communicate "truth," but sometimes with their own unique brand on it. Cities spawn suburbs, which are often later merged incestuously into the city. Historically, many nations have generated colonies in their own image, or have conquered neighboring nations and sought to impose their own laws and culture on the vanquished. Thus, we see varying forms of propagation at all levels of living systems. However they may choose to go about it, living systems attempt to propagate major features of themselves in other systems.

Environmental Control

In the broadest sense, maintenance, actualization, and propagation often involve attempts by living systems to control their environment. Business firms, for instance, try to protect themselves from harmful legislation by employing lobbyists and public relations experts to present the corporate viewpoint. Firms seek control of their markets through patents and advertising. Joint ventures, acquisitions, and mergers give them increased control over competition or resources. Internal growth allows them to become increasingly dominant in a given market or to protect themselves from market volatility through diversification.

By propagating their values to other systems, organizations make their environment more like themselves, thereby reducing unfriendly competition, generating reliable and congenial suppliers, producing loyal customers, and dominating markets. Through growth, organizations expand their boundaries and incorporate more of the environment within themselves. For the sake of maintenance, organizations act on their environment to avert threatening conditions before they become serious.

Note that the environment of a living system is not passive, although some components of it may be. The typical environment includes many other living systems, some smaller and some larger. Some of these external systems are sources of inputs, some are potential recipients of outputs, and some are coprocessors in the transformation process. Also, some external systems are threats as competitors, rivals for power, regulators, litigants, disrupters, or innovators. There are also nonliving threats such as floods, tornadoes, and drought.

A major part of a system's environment is its *suprasystem*, the next higher system of which it is a component or subsystem.[7] For instance, a business organization is a component either of a larger corporation or of the community or society in which it exists.

The suprasystem looms large in a business firm's environment because the firm is in a subordinate position. The firm is expected to accept values and instructions from its suprasystem. That does not prevent the firm from trying to exert upward influence, however. In the United States, this is often accomplished by means of lobbying and political campaign contributions.

Individuals and social systems generally try to protect themselves from what they perceive as excessive control by a suprasystem. In other words, living systems are proactive in trying to control their environment. They are not passive recipients of inputs and they do not assume that the environment will passively accept their outputs. In order to make life safer and more predictable, living systems constantly try to extend their control over elements of their environment. If possible, they incorporate these elements within themselves, making the "foreign" elements part of the system.

Critical Subsystems

Living systems must be able to perform certain critical processes in order to survive. They must possess or have access to *subsystems* that process matter, energy, and information. Subsystems are required for handling inputs, moving them through the system, storing and transforming them, and extruding outputs. Also required are subsystems that protect the system, hold it together, and allow it to move. Finally, a subsystem is needed to allow the system to propagate itself.

Miller identified twenty such *critical subsystems*.[8] They are listed and categorized in Table 1-1. Note that the critical subsystems can be roughly

Table 1-1
Twenty Critical Subsystems

I. SUBSYSTEMS WHICH PROCESS BOTH MATTER-ENERGY AND INFORMATION
1. Reproducer
2. Boundary

II. SUBSYSTEMS WHICH PROCESS MATTER-ENERGY	III. SUBSYSTEMS WHICH PROCESS INFORMATION
3. Ingestor	11. Input transducer
	12. Internal transducer
4. Distributor	13. Channel and net
	14. Timer
5. Converter	15. Decoder
6. Producer	16. Associator
7. Matter-energy storage	17. Memory
	18. Decider
	19. Encoder
8. Extruder } 9. Motor 10. Supporter	20. Output transducer

Source: Adapted from J. G. Miller and J. L. Miller, "Introduction: The nature of living systems," *Behavioral Science* 35 (1990): 159.

divided into two parallel sets, one for the processing of matter-energy and the other for information. Only the reproducer and boundary subsystems process both. However, all subsystems must work together under the direction of the template and the decider subsystem. Figure 1-1 presents a simplified picture of the twenty critical subsystems and some of the more important interconnections between them.

Figure 1-1
Simplified Schematic of the Critical Subsystems

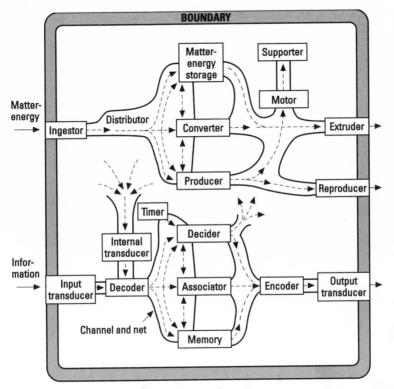

Two subsystems, in particular, tend to identify a living system: the *boundary* and the *decider*. From the point of view of an external observer, the boundary subsystem is often seen as defining the limits of the system. The boundary is at the *interface* between a system and its environment. If you cannot unambiguously determine whether something is within the boundary or not, then no clearly defined system exists.

In order to act purposefully every living system must have its own decider subsystem. The decider is the only subsystem whose functions cannot be dispersed to another system.[9] If a system cannot make its own decisions, it does not exist as a separate living entity, although it can live as a component of another system.

All members of an organization or other social system are part of its decider subsystem, so long as they make decisions based on the values, purposes, and goals of that system. When they make decisions based on their own values, however, they become deciders for themselves. Critical questions for social systems, therefore, are whether and when members are acting on behalf of the system rather than for themselves. These questions become especially important when we are talking about the top echelon of the decider subsystem, the leaders. For that reason, I will later devote most of Chapter 9 to this issue.

Summary of General Characteristics

All living systems possess certain general characteristics in common. For instance, each system

1. is composed primarily of protoplasm;
2. can exist only in an Earthlike environment;
3. contains a template that directs the development and functioning of its processes and structures;
4. is capable of maintaining itself, actualizing its potential, and propagating parts of itself or its template;
5. acts on its environment in order to reduce threats and improve the flow of inputs and outputs; and
6. contains or has access to twenty critical subsystems.

Miller persuasively demonstrates that these attributes are as true of groups, organizations, communities, societies, and supranational systems as they are of cells, organs, and organisms. Thus, he concludes that these are essential traits of any system that possesses life.[10]

People who take a superficial look at living systems theory often assume that it is simply an extended set of analogies between system levels. It is not. It is an attempt to identify the structures and processes that are common to all systems that display the properties of life. To the extent that these structures and processes are found at all levels, it can be assumed that they are essential features of the class of systems known as living systems.

Miller argues that the critical subsystems and other essential characteristics of life have spread from cells upward to the higher levels through a shred-out or fray-out process.[11] The primary method by which these characteristics spread from cells to organs and organisms is through increasing complexity of the genetic template. At the social system levels, however, the fray-out process involves learning and abstraction from the templates of lower levels in the development of memetic templates of increasing complexity.

There is no intent in living systems theory to deny the unique features of various forms and levels of life. At each level and even within levels, there are distinctive structures and processes called *emergents*. For instance, the use of symbols for communication emerges within the levels of organisms and continues at each higher level. Human individuals and social systems possess many emergent features that are not found in other living systems. Nonetheless, it is worthwhile to examine what we and our institutions have in common with other forms of life.

What you will discover, when you begin to look at groups and organizations as living systems, is that this viewpoint opens up new facets. A manager seeing the organization as a living entity will recognize new needs and will treat the organization differently than a manager who sees it as a tool or a possession. The manager's role moves from being a manipulative operator of a machine to serving as a decider and facilitator for a system that possesses its own history, values, purposes, and goals.

If you are not ready to look at organizations in this way, you may not wish to proceed further in this book. Everything from here on is built on the assumptions that organizations are living systems and that managers serve organizations in such processes as memory, association, and decision making. On the other hand, if you accept this viewpoint, the rest of the book will develop many specific ideas for acting on these assumptions.

OUTLINE OF THE CHAPTERS

Books on management often begin at the interpersonal level, proceed to management of groups, then to a strategy of the firm and its interaction with its environment. One of the advantages of the living systems viewpoint, however, is that there are many equivalencies between the levels of individuals, groups, organizations, communities, and societies. Thus, when we tackle a topic such as motivation, we may deal with motives of groups and of the organization at the same time that we discuss individual motives. The structure of this book utilizes this capability for multilevel analysis. For that reason, the book's structure may seem peculiar at first, but I am certain that you will see advantages in it.

We begin by looking at how organizations are founded, and in particular at the development of organizational templates. Thus, Chapter 2 is called "Managing the Birth of an Organization." It focuses, among other things, on choosing organizational values, purposes, and goals. Furthermore, it provides an overview of the critical processes that every organization requires for survival.

In order to activate the newborn organization we next deal with motivation. Chapter 3, called "Managing Motivation," shows how motivation is built on values, purposes, and goals, and is inextricably tied to decision making. The chapter analyzes the many points at which the motivation of one system can be influenced by other systems, but also emphasizes the two-way nature of motivational influence.

Managerial decisions must typically be implemented through other people and by use of other organizational resources. Notions of power and influence are developed in Chapter 4. Called "Managing Resources and Power," the chapter shows how power grows from possession or control of matter, energy, and information. It also explores the importance of exchange relationships, storage, and efficient use of resources.

Communication is essential for good decision making and implementation of decisions. Chapter 5, "Managing Information Flow," examines the information processes necessary for communication to occur, both within the organization and between the organization and its environment. The role of communication in influence processes is also analyzed. The concept of organizational learning is reviewed.

The link between information processes and production processes is emphasized in Chapter 6, "Managing Matter-Energy Flow." This chapter highlights managers' responsibilities for coordinating system processes, creating value, and ensuring effectiveness of the organization. Pathologies of matter-energy processing are studied.

Chapter 7, "Managing Internal Conflict and Stress," examines sources of conflict within organizations and surveys methods of conflict management, with special emphasis on negotiation.

Chapter 8 continues the focus on negotiation as a method of "Managing Environmental Relationships." It also examines the roles of managers in monitoring the environment, seeking favorable niches, and protecting the organization from attack. The importance of boundary and input/output processes is emphasized in this chapter. Ideas on designing immunity processes for organizations are discussed.

Chapter 9 takes an overall look at leadership and the decider subsystem. Managers face many difficulties in providing leadership for an organization and initiating change when it is necessary. Thus, the chapter is entitled "Managing Problems of Leadership."

Adaptation is the focus of Chapter 10, "Managing Change." Change is seen as inevitable; types of change are examined and many principles for dealing with change are developed. The chapter concludes with a discussion of organizational decline and renewal.

Chapter 11, "Managing the Future," looks at new organizational forms that are emerging, such as teleorganizations, multidomestic firms, and micro-organizations. It examines the question of whether disorganization is threatening our living organizations.

NOTES

1. For a more extensive description of these and other views of organizations, see Gareth Morgan, *Images of Organization* (Newbury Park, CA: Sage, 1986).

2. James G. Miller, *Living Systems* (New York: McGraw-Hill, 1978), 18.

3. Ibid., 34.

4. I am indebted to Dean Holt for this way of looking at organizations.

5. Miller, *Living Systems*, 18.

6. Richard Dawkins, *The Selfish Gene* (New York: Oxford University Press, 1976), 203–15.

7. Miller, *Living Systems*, 29.

8. Ibid., 51–87; James G. Miller and Jessie L. Miller, "Introduction: The nature of living systems," *Behavioral Science* 35 (1990): 157–63.

9. Miller, *Living Systems*, 32.

10. Ibid., 1.

11. Ibid., 1–4; Miller and Miller, "Introduction," 1–2.

Chapter 2

Managing the Birth of an Organization

Many managers never have an opportunity to give birth to an organization. That's a shame, because it is probably the most exciting part of management. If the essence of management is to make decisions and solve problems for an organization, you will never have a chance to make more important decisions than when you are trying to launch one.

If you are an entrepreneur, you may already have had the experience of putting together an organization. If you are a manager working for a large corporation, you may have the opportunity to open up a new plant, store, branch office, department, or division. Or you may at some point decide to go into business for yourself. Even if you never have to start an organization, however, there is much to be learned from thinking about the process.

Living systems theory is very helpful in planning the start-up of a new organization. The theory specifies the essential elements that must be in place for the newborn organization to survive and prosper. Let's take an example and see how living systems theory is applied.

A NEW BUSINESS

New business organizations are generated in a variety of ways. An existing firm may choose to expand into a new geographical area or a new product line, but such a venture may be seen as incompatible with the mission of the current organization or that organization may already be unwieldy. Thus, the firm decides to create a new division. Or perhaps, realizing that the new enterprise requires expertise that the firm does not possess, it forges a joint venture with another firm.

New organizations are also created by individuals or groups who have an idea—a novel product or service, an unexplored niche in the market, a cost-saving technology, a better method of delivery—and who decide to exploit it themselves. Perhaps they have the entrepreneurial spirit, or it may be that they have tried to sell their idea to existing firms and it has fallen on deaf ears. Organizations are also started by individuals who have no special idea but do have capital to invest. They may buy a franchise, for instance.

Let's take one of these scenarios and see what it means for an individual who must put the new organization together. We will first look at the situation of Terry Turner, who is an upper-level manager at UniGlobe, a large multinational conglomerate. Terry has just sold the chief executive officer (CEO) on developing a new line of products based on a technological breakthrough that the research and development (R&D) people have cooked up. The CEO says:

Since you're the one who championed this idea, I'm going to put you in charge of getting it off the ground. I don't think we can produce it in any of our existing plants, and it will involve selling to a whole new set of markets. We're going to have to set up a whole new subsidiary with its own production facilities and sales organization. This is too good an opportunity to pass up, but we'll have to move fast before our competitors get hold of it. I want to see plans and budgets for a start-up operation on my desk in one month. Let's call it Project NewVent. You can use your current staff to put it together. Let me know if you need any other resources.

Terry has just conceived a new organization, already code-named NewVent. Terry is one parent. The other is UniGlobe. Terry is an experienced executive, but has never started a new business before. Where should Terry begin?

Finding a Niche

Assuming that UniGlobe is prepared to finance the new operation, Terry's first concern is whether the new product idea will support a living organization. Is there an environmental niche for the organization? Every living system requires a supportive environment, meaning one that contains essential resources and can absorb the system's outputs, and one in which the competition is not too severe and the predators are not too fierce. If a living system cannot adjust to the stresses imposed on it by its environment, it cannot survive.[1]

Incubation. A newborn organization, even with the best planning, is relatively weak and defenseless. It will require a nurturing environment until it gains strength. That is why business incubators have become popular.[2] They serve the same purpose for newborn businesses that other incubators serve for human infants or baby chicks.

In a business incubator, a larger system, for instance a university or municipality, provides certain essential resources, such as temporary space, secretarial help, bookkeeping, legal aid, tax advice, and expert business consultation. Incubators are not for everyone, however. They typically focus on high-tech or innovative ventures that have few, if any, direct competitors. If you are starting another pizza restaurant, even with a new twist, an incubator will not help you.

NewVent does not require an incubator. The mother corporation will provide protection and essential services during the gestation period and for a while after start-up. But Terry must maintain confidence among the corporation's leaders that NewVent will eventually make a worthwhile contribution to corporate goals. If those leaders sense that the new division may never be profitable, or if UniGlobe itself comes under financial pressure, they may be quick to jettison the new venture. Organizational abortion and infanticide are rather common in the corporate world.

Even if the new organization has a protector, it must generally also have a market for its product or service, adequate working capital, good sources of materials and machinery, a ready supply of labor, available transport, and some form of advertising. In other words:

Viewing the organization as an open system, it requires inputs of money, labor, technology, materials, machinery, and orders, and its processes must create outputs that have value to other systems. Each of these requirements is a constraint on the viability of the proposed organization.

Market. Often the most difficult constraint to satisfy is the need for clients or customers. Someone must want what the firm can produce; they must want it enough to pay more than the firm's costs of production; and there must be enough such people to sustain a steady cycle of business that will support the organization.

We may think we have a good product or service, but does anyone else think so? It is worth our time to seek an answer to that question before we invest anything else in the business.

Advertising can help to create a market, but there must be a basic need to build on. Does our brainchild satisfy a need better than any existing product or service? Or does it satisfy a new need, one that the customers may not even be aware of?

Who are the potential customers? Are they individuals, families, other businesses, government agencies? How many potential customers are there? How often might they need our product or service? How much money do they have to spend?

Is the use of our product or service seasonal? Are there laws or customs that might restrict the use of it? How quickly may competitors enter the market with a similar offering? All of these questions and many more might be asked in trying to estimate the potential market.

Resources. Resource constraints may also be critical. If our idea requires a new material, or machinery that no one is producing yet, or a skill that is rare, we face the daunting task of changing part of the firm's environment before we can commence. Many good ideas founder at this point. For instance, in 1945 Arthur C. Clarke, author of *2001: A Space Odyssey,* developed and published the idea of using satellites in geosynchronous orbits for communication networks, but could not patent it because the technology for boosting such satellites into orbit did not then exist. By the time the necessary hardware was developed, his idea was in the public domain.[3]

Money is a critical resource, of course. Probably more young businesses, especially those founded by individuals, fail because of inadequate financing than for any other reason. But often the financing is inadequate because potential investors, banks, or corporate leaders are not convinced that a sufficient market exists.

For the moment, NewVent does not have a money problem, although eventually Terry is going to have to convince UniGlobe to shell out the funds necessary for a new plant. To illustrate the problems an entrepreneur might face in obtaining this critical resource, let's look at another case.

Alex Montero is currently trying to obtain a franchise from Virtual Realty, a nationwide network of realtors. It is a service business based on the technologies of electronic communication and virtual reality. Using interactive video equipment, potential clients in distant cities are able to "walk" through the houses being offered in a certain locale. They can also hear the sales pitch, smell the freshly baked bread, and feel the warmth of the fireplace. They can even ask questions and receive prerecorded answers.

Alex has only half of the capital needed to obtain the franchise. Because the technology is new and the local realty market is already crowded, Alex faces difficulties in convincing a bank to lend the rest of the money. Thus, Alex has asked a friend, Chris Torborg, to become a partner in the business. Although Chris is currently very involved with her own business, Alex is only asking for financial help, not her managerial expertise.

After a demonstration of the video technology, Chris is impressed with its potential, but concerned that it may add too much cost. She insists that, if she is going to invest in Alex's venture, it must be on a proper business basis. Alex must produce a detailed business plan, including specification of goals; estimates of market size, capital requirements, cash flow, and profits; and a timetable of specific steps for development of the business.

Alex complains that the banks required the same sort of information. They also wanted to know about the success record of other Virtual Realty franchisees. But Chris is insistent, so Alex puts together a business plan and returns with it to renew the offer of a partnership. Alex finally convinces Chris with the argument that clients will be willing to pay more for this service because they save money and time with fewer house-hunting trips. She agrees that such a service would have added value. Chris and Alex sign a partnership agreement. Montero Virtual Realty (MVR) is born.

Choosing a niche. Assuming that necessary resources exist and there are markets for our idea, we may have the further task of choosing among possibilities. For instance, should MVR specialize in residential or commercial properties? If it chooses residential properties, should it strive for the high end of the housing market and a small, exclusive group of customers, or for the lower-priced mass housing market? The expensive technology that MVR plans to use, as well as the nature of the network it is joining, push it toward the high-end residential market.

Terry has similar questions at NewVent. Should the firm locate close to its customers, its suppliers, corporate headquarters, or a source of highly skilled or cheap labor? Should it aim initially for the original equipment market or the replacement market? The answers to such questions depend on the nature of the basic idea and the key constraints it faces.

Choosing the right niche from among those that are available may make the difference between a long, prosperous life and an early demise for an organization.

Unfortunately, although living systems theory stresses the importance of the environment and can give you some idea of what to look for, the task of choosing a niche is still largely an art.

Creating the Template

Assuming that Terry has identified a niche for NewVent, the next task is to develop a design for the organization. As I noted in Chapter 1, every living system must have a template consisting of a set of instructions for developing and maintaining the basic structure and processes of the system.

New organisms are produced, in most cases, by the mating of parent organisms. The genetic templates of the progeny are automatically determined by this mating process. Organizations, on the other hand, may be germinated by an individual, a group, an organization, a community, a society, a supranational system, or any combination of these systems. The template for an organization may be based on the template of the parent system, on the founder's prior experience, or on a wholly new design. Indeed, a new organization design might be the basic idea from which the organization grows.

Whatever the source of the template may be, there are certain structures and processes that must be specified.

> The template should indicate what kind of organization is to be built (e.g., for-profit or nonprofit; manufacturing, marketing, or service; regional or national; partnership or corporation); its initial size and plans for growth; its basic values, purposes, and goals; and its decision-making structure.

The business plan that Alex was required to produce for MVR is a start on the template for the realty firm. Although the template may be modified later, it must exist at the origin of the system.

The most visible part of the template is often a written document, such as a corporate charter or business plan. In the case of a franchise such as Virtual Realty, it may include a thick book of instructions on procedures. NewVent, on the other hand, will probably draw much of its template from the policies and procedures of UniGlobe. Yet the initial plan may also reside entirely in the memory of the founder, as is frequently the case with individual entrepreneurs.

For organizations, the template consists of two parts: the genes of the organization's members, specifying their physical and mental capabilities and innate values, and a set of ideas or memes, including values, purposes, goals, structures, and processes. Some of these ideas are created specifically for the organization; others are carried into the organization by the members. The key member and carrier of memes is, of course, the founder of the organization. Nevertheless, anyone else inducted into the organization will bear genetic characteristics and ideas that may influence its structure and processes, especially during the early, formative stages.

> If the founders of an organization wish to maximize their influence on its design, they must specify the template as fully as possible before bringing other people in. To do so, they must anticipate what sorts of instructions the organization will need.

NewVent is to be involved in the manufacture of magnetic flanges for the automobile industry. Initially, magnetic flanges will be introduced in the most expensive car models. The market is expected to expand gradually into the less expensive lines as costs decrease and customers become more familiar with the product's advantages.

Terry anticipates starting with 30 employees and $11.5 million in capital investment, growing to 120 employees and $35 million after 2 years. The division is expected to break even after 18 months and achieve a return on investment of 15 percent after 5 years. Ten percent of gross profits will be ploughed back into research. NewVent aims to dominate the new market for magnetic flanges, achieving and maintaining a 60 percent share. Employees will receive annual bonuses based on profits, and so forth.

If this were an independent corporation, you would need some other specifications. For instance, you might allow debt to be no more than 50 percent of your financing, but no less than 20 percent. The corporation might be governed by a Board of Directors consisting of six people elected from among the stockholders, with yourself as chairperson. The board might be required to meet at least twice a year to review operations and set basic policies. You might be designated to serve as CEO.

All of these elements and much more can and should be specified before financing is sought or anyone is hired. Indeed, many of these specifications are required in the prospectus for any stock offering, as well as by banks before they will lend any money and by corporate boards before they will approve expansion plans.

The great variety of specifications and instructions required in the template of a new organization should not be surprising if we consider that organizations are more complex than the groups and individuals of which they are composed. It took Mother Nature millions of years to develop the genetic template for human beings. In organizations we are attempting to build on that foundation. We are designing a system to accomplish things that no individual could do alone, and we are attempting to complete the design in a few days or months rather than millenia.

The task is daunting, and it is often done poorly. Fortunately, living systems theory can help us by specifying the critical structures and processes that must be in place for any living organization.

CRITICAL PROCESSES

As we noted in Chapter 1, a living system must either possess each of twenty critical subsystems or else must be associated with other systems that possess them. The critical subsystems themselves, and the structures associated with them in a typical organization, are discussed at length in Chapters 5 and 6. The key point for our purposes here is that these critical subsystems provide a set of essential processes. The list of processes that must be carried out will aid us in designing the template for a new organization.

Table 2-1 lists all of the known critical processes of a living system and the subsystem to which each process belongs. In order to survive, grow, and propagate, all living systems must be able to carry out these critical processes. If a system does not possess the means to perform a critical process by itself, it must be able to disperse the process to another system.

Let us take each process in turn and see what the organizational template might say about it. I will begin with the reproducer, because it puts the new system together.

Reproducer Process

Transmitting the template. The *reproducer* process transmits template information from an existing living system to a new one. If NewVent is successful, it may at some point wish to spin off new organizations in its image. Initially, however, Terry is more concerned with transmitting template information *to* NewVent. For this purpose Terry, along with anyone else who may be allowed to give advice, will take over this process for the organization.

Terry and UniGlobe are the basic sources of NewVent's template information. In writing a business plan Terry is attempting to transmit this basic information first to the CEO and the board, then to potential employees, stockholders, creditors, customers, and government agencies, as well as to NewVent's archives.

Under other circumstances of birth other modes of transmission may predominate. In the case of a franchise such as MVR, much of the writing of the template has already been done by the central organization. It might be transmitted by means of written policies and procedures, by training programs for new managers, and by use of standard hardware and software. In a joint venture or partnership, on the other hand, the template would probably be formulated by negotiation between the partners in the enterprise, with each party transmitting its values in an attempt to influence the shape of the organization.

Assembling components. Terry must also assemble the components of the new system. The template should specify what is needed initially in terms of number of employees, skills, working capital, buildings, machinery, furniture, energy conduits, communications equipment, and so forth. Specifications are required for both the quantity and the quality of these components, as well as their expected date of acquisition, useful life, and schedule of maintenance. The template should also indicate how these requirements are expected to change over time, so that the system can plan the acquisition of additional resources as well as the disposal of excess or obsolete components.

Granted, this is a tall order; Terry may not be able to anticipate all of these requirements. Nonetheless, *a manager should try to specify as much as*

Table 2-1
Critical Subsystems and Critical Processes of a Living System

Subsystem	Process
Reproducer	Transmit template information for a new system Assemble matter-energy to compose the new system Assist the new system until it becomes self-supporting
Boundary	Contain and bind together the system's components Protect the components from environmental stresses Exclude or permit entry to matter-energy and information
Ingestor	Bring matter-energy across the boundary from the environment
Distributor	Carry matter-energy around the system to each component
Converter	Change inputs into forms more useful to the system
Producer	Form stable, enduring associations among inputs
Storage	Hold deposits of various sorts of matter-energy
Extruder	Transmit matter-energy out of the system
Motor	Move the system or parts of it in relation to environment Move components of environment in relation to each other
Supporter	Maintain a proper spatial relationship among components
Input transducer	Bring markers bearing information into the system Change them into forms that transmit within the system
Internal transducer	Receive markers from subsystems or system components Change them into forms that transmit within the system
Channel and net	Carry information-bearing markers around the system
Timer	Generate and transmit timing signals to decider subsystems
Decoder	Alter the code of information input into a private code
Associator	Form enduring associations among items of information
Memory	Store, maintain, and retrieve information-bearing markers
Decider	Establish purposes and goals for the system Receive information inputs from all other subsystems Analyze inputs, synthesize plans, and choose a plan Transmit information outputs that implement the choice
Encoder	Alter code of information from private to public code
Output transducer	Change system's markers into other forms of matter-energy Transmit markers bearing information from the system

possible in the template, if only to establish the categories that should be covered. Details can be changed later based on experience.

Assistance. In some cases, a new system requires assistance until it becomes self-supporting. Providing such aid is an additional responsibility of the reproducer. In the case of NewVent, the parent corporation appears ready to supply the necessary capital and other services, and is willing to give the division a grace period before it is expected to show a profit.

Alex and Chris, in order to get MVR over the initial hump, expect to forego any distribution of profits for a few years. In addition, they will initially draw little or no compensation for their time, and may lend some of their property or other resources to the enterprise. Other organizations, such as a business incubator, a franchising network, a large customer that wants the firm's product or service, or a vendor that is willing to delay payment in the hopes of future orders, may also furnish elements of the reproducer process.

The reproducer processes of the parents provide a new system with its original template. In addition to the template, the critical processes that most clearly define a living system are those associated with its boundary and decider. Let us now look at these processes.

Boundary Process

Containment. The first task of the *boundary* process is to contain the system's components and bind them together. In the case of an organization such as NewVent, containment is accomplished primarily by walls and fences. The buildings and grounds that surround the organization also contain most of its members, at least during their working hours, as well as machinery, furniture, and other equipment belonging to the organization. Guards, guard dogs, and gates may also take part in this process, particularly if theft of equipment and materials is a serious problem.

Cohesiveness. Although containment can be a critical matter for security-conscious organizations, binding the components together is a more general concern. Organizational cohesiveness and loyalty have become key management issues, because they are tied to quality of production and service. Your plan for NewVent should indicate how such binding forces will be generated.

Most managers recognize that members do not automatically identify with the organization and its goals. Some of the steps often taken to create and maintain such identification are

1. *recruit and select new members on the basis of their agreement with the values and goals of the organization;*

2. *provide orientation for new members in organizational values, goals, and policies;*
3. *expose members to ceremonies, stories, and language that support and emphasize key organizational values;* and
4. *dispense rewards for loyalty and penalties, including discharge, for disloyalty.*

Protection. Another element of the boundary process is to protect components from environmental stress. To put it simply, the boundary keeps good things in and bad things out. Protection is partly a matter of designing and maintaining buildings so that they can protect people and equipment from stressors such as fire, flood, wind, earthquake, heat, cold, and air pollution. For the people, however, environmental stress also comes in forms such as economic downturns, weak or excessive consumer demand, high taxes, poorly performing schools, decaying communities, threats and actualities of war, expensive and/or inadequate medical care, legal problems, debt, and family conflict.

An organization such as NewVent cannot protect its members from most of these stressors, but it can provide a supportive environment that offers temporary relief from some of them. Employees often find that the social relationships at work provide a haven from stressful relationships at home, for instance. The workplace can also offer opportunities to discuss problems with others who are in the same boat, so that they realize the distress is shared. A good organizational plan includes times and places for such discussion. It also provides means for addressing problems about which the organization often *can* do something, such as drug and alcohol abuse.

Screening. The boundary is also responsible for permitting entry to various forms of matter-energy and information, but excluding those forms that might be harmful to the system. In trying to cope with drug and alcohol abuse, for instance, NewVent could (1) ban illegal drugs and alcoholic beverages from company property; (2) enforce the ban with inspections and drug testing; (3) screen job applicants, rejecting those with a history of substance abuse; and (4) provide a detoxification program for existing employees who are willing to seek help.

In general, keeping harmful material and information out of the organization involves:

1. identifying *what is potentially harmful to the system;*
2. detecting *these harmful forms of matter-energy and information;*
3. excluding *them, either by preventing them from entering the system or by ejecting them after they enter;* and
4. isolating *or* transforming *harmful materials that cannot be excluded.*

For instance, if a firm decides that it would be harmed by customers who are poor credit risks, it might subscribe to a service that lists such risky customers, set up a computer screening system that will match new customers with the list, and reject orders from any customers so identified. Likewise, to protect the firm's computer system from viruses, it might install an automatic screening program for incoming data and software, designed to detect known viruses and purge them from the system.

The boundary must also screen outputs. NewVent must be able to protect itself from the theft of products, materials, tools, and trade secrets. The last point may be particularly critical, because the division's supposed competitive advantage is based on new technology. To maintain a reputation for quality, NewVent must likewise screen its output of products or services. To protect its public image, it may carefully monitor communications with the press. Furthermore, it may be required to filter its effluents, removing pollutants and treating them.

Maturity. Large, mature firms have some natural advantages with respect to protection from the environment. Typically, they possess their own property, rather than having to lease and share premises with others. They may also have a cadre of defensive specialists, such as lawyers, human resource managers, computer system experts, purchasing agents, and industrial hygienists. Furthermore, they will have retained earnings, established sources of credit, and steady markets to ease some of the financial fluctuations.

A new organization attached to a mature firm is lucky because it can draw on the defensive resources of the parent. Likewise, a franchising system such as Virtual Realty may provide training in methods of avoiding or countering harmful situations.

There is no way that small, young, independent firms can duplicate these advantages by themselves; such firms are inherently more vulnerable. With awareness of the problem and good planning, however, they can reduce their vulnerability. What is called for is good decision making about the start-up phase of the organization.

The need to protect a new organization from environmental stress is often overlooked in the design stage. Entrepreneurs tend to be so focused on offense, that is, getting their product or service into the market, that they forget about defense. Frequently, the unfortunate result is that the fledgling firm fails even though it finds a market. It falls victim to such unanticipated stresses as poorly trained employees, pilferage, difficulty in obtaining raw materials, loss of trade secrets, undercutting by competitors, failure to adhere to government regulations, and refusal of customers to pay on time.

Decider Process

Establishing purposes and goals. The *decider process* for an organization consists of all of the decision making that is done in accordance with the values, purposes, and goals of the organization. The first stage of the decider process is to establish purposes and goals for the system, if they are not already specified by the template.

Purposes, in Miller's terminology, are specific preferred internal steady states or targets.[4] An example for NewVent would be the specification of the initial number of employees and subsequent growth in size of the division. These figures provide specific targets for decisions to advertise job openings and process applications.

Other targets that might be specified in the template include desired profit levels for a series of accounting periods, a minimum level of cash flow, amounts of compensation allocated to employees, size of plant and amounts of various kinds of machinery required, advertising budgets, and pricing schedules. Less precise targets might deal with topics such as employee satisfaction, the firm's reputation for quality and on-time delivery, and a commitment to developing new products.

Goals are external targets. They might include expected sales levels per time period, numbers of new and repeat customers, return rate of defective products, degree of compliance with government regulations, amount of allowable atmospheric pollution, energy usage rates, cost and quality of raw materials, and quantity and quality of job applicants.

Some of these targets might normally be found in a corporate charter, prospectus, or business plan, along with a broader statement of purposes such as "manufacturing high quality magnetic flanges at a competitive price" and goals such as "attaining a dominant position in the magnetic flange market." Other mentioned targets would seldom be found in writing, but perhaps ought to be. The point is:

Managers should be as specific as they can about as many purposes and goals as they can think of. Goals and purposes serve as guides to everyday decision making. Having a variety of them protects managers from overemphasizing one particular target.

Even if put in writing, purposes and goals are not carved in stone. They can be modified on the basis of experience; indeed, they can be dynamic from the start, indicating expected growth over time. If we do not specify them in the template, however, we probably will not think to modify them later.

Receiving and analyzing information. The second stage of the decider process consists of receiving and analyzing information inputs from all other subsystems and the environment. Analysis includes assessing the relevance of information, calculating the extent of deviations from targets, and noting what *adjustment processes* are available for correcting deviations.

The template can help this stage by specifying who, or what positions, in the organization are responsible for (1) gathering what information and from whom and (2) analyzing it. Thus, the template might indicate that engineers and research personnel will maintain professional contacts and read the technical literature in order to remain current with new materials and technology. The sales department, on the other hand, will be charged with the task of listening to customers, finding out what they want, and transmitting that information to the product designers. Unfortunately, such specifications are often missing in the template of a new organization, and even of mature ones, with the result that vital information is not collected or is not transmitted to those who could use it.

Synthesis and choice. The third stage of the decider process consists of synthesizing and choosing plans of action. Synthesis consists of combining existing alternatives and devising new ones.

The template should indicate (1) how choices will be made and (2) who will make them with respect to various fields of action. For instance, analysis of market data and synthesis of marketing programs might be carried out by a committee of marketing managers with the final choice being made by majority vote or consensus of the committee, or by fiat of the vice president for marketing.

Care should be taken in delineating the process of synthesis and choice, because it can make a very substantial difference in outcomes. Whatever the desired decision process is, specifying it in the template will clarify lines of responsibility and authority.

Implementation. Clear lines of authority will also aid the last stage of the decider process, namely, transmitting commands or suggestions for implementation. The template should indicate how commands are transmitted (e.g., orally, in writing, or by computer), the proper nodes through which they are transmitted (e.g., through managers and supervisors or directly from the decision level to those who will implement the orders), and normal time limits for implementation. It is also wise to specify a method for monitoring processes and outcomes, with a feedback loop for control.

Division of the decider process into four stages might seem to imply that decision making must proceed through each stage separately and in order. As we see in Chapter 3, however, the stages often occur simultaneously or in iterative fashion. That is, we may set goals at the same time that we choose a course of action, or we may alter our purposes after gathering information. Implementation may include the process of collecting data for the purpose of feedback and control. The point is that deciding includes all four stages, not that they must occur in sequence.

As we see in Chapter 9, the decider process is the source of some of the most severe problems in management. Proper specification of the process in the template can go a long way toward alleviating these problems. But the decision process also requires good information and proper implementation. Thus, it depends on the proper functioning of other subsystems. Let us look first at the processes that supply information to, and convey commands from, the decider.

Information Inputs and Outputs

Information is carried by physical *markers* of matter-energy. Information is contained in patterns of differences or changes in matter-energy, such as the patterns of black and white matter on this page, or the patterns of change in air pressure (i.e., waves) that carry sound to our ears.

When information is processed by a living system, it may convey *meaning* to that system. Meaningful information causes some change in the system, although that change may be minimal, such as adding the information to memory.

In organizations, it is worthwhile to separate information into two types. The first is functional information communicated between persons, from person to machine and vice versa, or from machine to machine for the purpose of controlling and coordinating processes. The second type is money and money equivalents (e.g., accounting entries, checks, trade goods) used for the purposes of keeping score and facilitating exchange.

In some organizations, money—the bottom line—assumes so great an importance that the functional type of information is largely ignored. For instance, meeting the budget and using all allocated funds becomes more important than efficiency, quality, and productivity. Young organizations, on the other hand, sometimes forget about the need to make a profit in the rush to develop new products and markets. Obviously, a business plan should reflect balanced concern for both kinds of information.

Information intake. Information comes from two sources: the environment and the subsystems. Information about the environment has to be brought across the boundary. This task is carried out by the *input transducer* process, which brings markers bearing information into the system. For example, our senses pick up external information in the form of sights, sounds, tastes, odors, and textures. Members of an organization, acting as the input transducers for the organization, receive information in such forms as money, customers' comments, telephone inquiries, letters of complaint, government regulations, and economic forecasts.

Internal information. Information also comes from within the system. A person's *internal transducer* receives markers from subsystems or components through receptors for pain, pressure, heat, and pleasure. Within an organization the members act as internal transducers, receiving markers that may indicate, for instance, strain within a department or the current status of a process. Internal audits and job satisfaction surveys are also part of this process.

Input and internal transducers also change the original markers into forms that can be transmitted within the system. For instance, our nervous system uses electrochemical markers, not the markers of light and sound that convey words to our senses. Our eyes and ears must convert patterns of light and sound into electrochemical signals. We may also require *artifacts* to help us, such as a telephone to change electronic signals into sound.

Information output. Output *transducers* transmit information-bearing markers out of the system. In the process the system's markers are changed into forms that can be transmitted in the environment. For example, after forming a business plan for NewVent, Terry must transmit parts of this plan to the CEO, the Board of Directors, employees, customers, and so forth.

> *It is often critical that managers choose the right media (i.e., forms of markers) for the message. A written message has staying power, for instance, whereas an oral message may initially have greater force but is more quickly forgotten. In designing an organization, managers should consider who will speak for the firm to the outside world, and what they may speak about.*

Carrying information. Once information is received and changed into an appropriate form of marker, it enters the *channel and net* process. This process carries markers around the system to other components and subsystems. In organizations, the channel and net consists, at times, of all of the members plus artifacts such as computer networks, intercoms, and mail carts.

In designing the channel and net process, you must consider such factors as speed of transmission, expected volume of information flow, quality of information required, and interruption of other processes. For instance, do you want machine operators to "drop everything" in order to receive new instructions, or can the message wait until they finish a process? Do you require a two-way channel that allows for clarification of messages and full participation in decision making, or is a one-way channel such as a written memo sufficient and more efficient? Do you want a channel that can carry large volumes of quantitative data, or one such as face-to-face contact that permits a greater variety of markers to be used? Do you want a network that permits everyone in the organization to communicate with everyone else, or would a more limited network be more efficient and effective?

The choices are numerous and difficult, which explains why many organizations employ expert consultants to design their information networks. Chapter 5 has more to say about the design of information processing subsystems.

Deciders are linked to the channel and net. The difference between deciders and *nodes* is that deciders choose what information to pass on, whereas nodes pass on information without any deliberate change. Of course, errors and noise may be introduced in either case.

In designing the channel and net process, managers must anticipate distortion and try to provide ways to overcome it. Multiple channels (e.g., backing up a phone call with a memo) and appeal systems are a couple of the means often used.

Decoding and encoding. Messages in the channel and net often require decoding before they can be understood. The digital code used by computers must be changed into numbers and words. A letter in a foreign language must be translated. Government documents written in "bureaucratese" and jargon-infested scientific papers must be turned into plain English. Altering the code of information input into the private code of the system is the task of the *decoder* process.

The *encoder* reverses the process, altering the private code of the system into one that can be interpreted by other systems. The encoder, together with the output transducer, allows the decider to transmit information outside of the system.

Decoding and encoding information in an organization is a technical process. In organizations, the process is normally carried out by people who have special expertise. The main concern, as the plan is developed, is that the organization has, or has access to, people who can do the necessary decoding and encoding. Failure to respond to a government regulation because the organization lacks people who can interpret it would be a serious error, for instance. Likewise, inability to communicate with a customer in terms that the customer can understand is likely to lose the sale.

Timing. It has recently been recognized that a *timer* process is needed to provide information about time and rate.[5] This information is transmitted to the decider of the system and to deciders of subsystems so that behavior can be paced and coordinated chronologically. This process is aided in organizations by clocks, calendars, paced conveyor belts, bells and whistles, and computer processing speed.

Although timing is largely a mechanical process, there are at least two concerns that deserve some planning. One concern is the general pace of the system; should everyone be frantically busy or is it better to proceed at a more relaxed pace that allows time for reflection? Should deadlines be tight, loose, or flexible? Can some parts of the system operate at a more rapid pace than others?

The second concern is for coordination between components. If the processes of the organization are complex and highly interrelated, devices such as PERT charts and computerized scheduling algorithms will be needed to coordinate activities. Otherwise, the efficiency of the system will be constrained by bottlenecks.

Learning processes. The *associator* and *memory* processes together provide the system with the ability to learn. The associator links items of information together. A simple example would be the association of two simultaneous stimuli, such as the taste and aroma of an apple, which together give you a different impression of the apple than either stimulus alone would. On the other hand, the association is often between an external stimulus and an item stored in memory, as when a new piece of information about a customer gives a more complete picture of their needs. The association of bits of information creates new information.

The associator process in organizations is generally dispersed to the individual members, although computers can be programmed to do some simple associating. A firm such as NewVent depends on its employees at all levels to make associations and learn as they work.

It should be made clear to employees that learning for the organization is part of their job.

To have a long-lasting effect, associations must be stored in memory. The memory process consists of storing information-bearing markers, maintaining them, and retrieving them. Our brains do this through electrochemical processes.

One of the things that differentiates human beings from other animals is our ability to augment memory with such devices as writing, photography, and magnetic recording. Organizations employ files, archives, and various forms of computer memory to aid the memories of the members. The plan should indicate what memory aids will be used.

Innovating. Innovation comes from the associator and memory processes. Many managers make the mistake of deliberately trying to limit the amount of innovating that lower-level employees do, by introducing standardized procedures that are to be followed regardless of information input. This not only wastes a basic capability of the employees, it also prevents the organization from learning better procedures or adapting to circumstances.

A young organization like NewVent, which is feeling its way in an uncertain world, especially needs to utilize the associator and memory processes of its employees. A good way to do this is to make it explicit to them that finding better ways to do things is part of their jobs. Some control over innovation has to be exercised, of course, but it should not be done in a way that implies innovation is wrong.

Innovation, because it involves not only thinking of better processes or better products but also putting the ideas into effect, is a link between information processing and matter-energy processing. Let us now look at the critical subsystems that process matter-energy.

Matter-Energy Processes

Ingestion. As with information, the first task is to bring matter and energy across the boundary into the system. This process is carried out by the *ingestor* process. Ingestion is a relatively simple process in most organizations, requiring only that inputs are officially received, logged in or metered, and put into the distributor subsystem to be carried to the right person or department. The process usually involves many of the same people and departments that serve the boundary function of screening inputs. The plan simply needs to make it clear that these people have responsibility for the ingestor process.

Ejection. In terms of personnel or departments the ingestor process may be combined with the *extruder* process, which ejects products and wastes across the boundary into the environment. NewVent must have people or departments responsible for shipping products and properly disposing of wastes such as scrap metal and polluted water. Water treatment plants, trash compactors, pulverizers, dumpsters, sewer lines, and smokestacks aid the process.

Young organizations often pay little attention to the extruder process, especially waste disposal. They make good products but forget to ship them on time. They design high-quality services, but are slipshod about how they deliver them. They let wastes pile up and interfere with efficient production. And they pollute the environment until government regulators descend on them.

Thorough design of the extruder process should be part of the plan from the start. The extruder process must also be coordinated with the output transducer by means of marketing and sales plans.

Internal distribution. The *distributor* process is responsible for carrying matter and energy around the system to each component. Although artifacts together with certain people, such as clerks and forklift operators, are primarily responsible for distribution, at times any member of the organization may become involved in the process.

Efficient production of goods and services, as well as prompt shipment of finished products, requires a distributor that delivers on time in the right quantities. Thus, the timer and decider processes are intimately involved in controlling the distributor process.

Conversion and production. The *converter* and *producer* processes are the heart of many business organizations. The converter breaks down matter and energy into simpler forms whereas the producer synthesizes matter and energy into more complex forms. In either case, the resulting "product" has enhanced worth to the system or its trading partners.

The basic idea that led to the formation of NewVent may have been a better converter or producer process. On the other hand, some conversion and production is commonly dispersed to other organizations. For instance, most firms rely on utilities to supply electric power, and many subcontract out at least part of the production process. In any case, these processes are seldom overlooked in the plans for a new organization. Even a service agency such as MVR must plan how best to utilize the energy of its sales force.

Because production planning is highly technical and is well covered elsewhere, we do not focus on it in this book. However, techniques such as total quality management (TQM) integrate production planning with other system processes. These links are examined in Chapter 6.

Storage. The flow of matter and energy through a living system is never absolutely steady. There are times when matter or energy must be held for future use. This need is met by the *storage* process.

Storage consists of three stages: (1) insertion, (2) maintenance, and (3) retrieval. In organizations, the process may involve people in areas such as raw materials and finished products inventory and the tool crib, as well as a variety of artifacts. (Note: artifacts associated with each of the critical processes are discussed in Chapters 5 and 6.)

Moving and supporting. The *motor* and *supporter* processes complete the list of essential processes. The motor moves the system or parts of it in relation to its environment, or moves components of its environment in relation to each other. For instance, MVR provides its salespeople with automobiles to enable them to show homes to clients. NewVent needs a fleet of trucks to deliver supplies or products.

A planning concern with respect to the motor process is the availability of fast, efficient, and/or inexpensive service. Is it better to try to provide your own motor capability or to rely on other systems such as trucking firms and public transportation?

The supporter maintains a proper spatial relationship among components of the system. The facilities housing an organization provide most of its supporter process. Young organizations typically pay little attention to this process. Rather, people move freely within the organization and the lines between functions are blurred.

Assuming that it is desirable to encourage freedom of movement at this stage of development, look for facilities that have few walls or floors separating the employees. If there are certain functions, such as accounting, that should be kept separate, locate them in an office by themselves, or even a different building.

Other Processes?

The critical processes listed here are required by all living systems. However, there may well be processes that are necessary for organizations but not required by individuals. There may also be processes that aid the performance of an organization, even if they are not essential to its survival.

For instance, communication seems to assume greater importance in organizations and other social systems than it does for individuals. Communication involves the input and output transducers, encoder and decoder, channel and net, associator, memory, and decider subsystems. Thus, it is already subsumed among the processes we have discussed. If we wish to consider it as a unitary process, however, its importance to organizations can be understood from the fact that decision making is more widely dispersed in organizations than it is in individuals or groups. Because communication poses some particular difficulties for organizations, it is discussed in depth in Chapter 5.

Of necessity, the critical processes have been treated very briefly in this chapter. The intent was to give an overview of the complexity of the system and a first look at some of the details with which a manager must cope. If you think something has been left out of the picture, you may find that it is covered in a later chapter.

SUMMARY

Utilizing certain basic concepts of living systems theory, I have tried to indicate the importance of taking time for thorough planning before you try to start a new organization. Living systems are extremely complex, consisting of a large number of closely interrelated processes and structures. It is foolish to think that an entrepreneur can just find a little money, collect a few people, feed them a good idea, and a viable organization will emerge—although I admit that short-run profits may be made that way.

First of all, the idea may not be as good as it seems. It should be tested in order to find out whether there is really a niche for the new enterprise. Will there be sufficient customers to support the firm? Can adequate raw materials and labor be found? Do others already have a head start? The founder's first task, after developing an idea that might provide a suitable market niche, is to check on whether that niche can support the firm. Don't expect a definitive answer to that question until you actually put together an organization and try it, but don't start out blindly either.

The second task, as I have indicated, is to develop a template—a charter and business plan for the organization. This is a very elaborate and critical task, one that is typically not done well. Many young organizations muddle through by continually modifying and augmenting the template as they go, but they could get off to a much quicker and healthier start if the founder(s) would take the time to write a thorough plan at the beginning. Even if that plan must be modified later, the factors that must be changed are easier to locate.

The reasons that writing a template is difficult are contained in the recitation of critical processes. There are dozens of processes and subprocesses that must be carried out in order for the organization to survive. Structures must be provided to carry out each of these processes, or else there must be a plan for dispersing processes to other systems. Furthermore, the processes must be integrated and coordinated by the key process of decision making.

The template is a set of preset decisions that, if they are made well, greatly simplify and accelerate the ad hoc decisions of day-to-day operations. That is why franchises are often worth the money paid for them. They provide a pretested template that has withstood the natural selection processes of the market place.

Do not take lightly the task of writing a charter and business plan for any new organization. Use the list of critical processes as a checklist to ensure that you have not forgotten important parts of the system, and that the parts are properly coordinated. But do not forget that, no matter how well you perform the task initially, you must allow for modification of the template as the organization grows and the environment changes.

NOTES

1. James G. Miller, *Living Systems* (New York: McGraw-Hill, 1978), 18.

2. David N. Allen and Syedur Rahman, "Small business incubators: A positive environment for entrepreneurship," *Journal of Small Business Management* 23, no. 3 (1985): 12–22.

3. Neil McAleer, *Odyssey: The Authorised Biography of Arthur C. Clarke* (London: Victor Gollanz Ltd., 1992), 58–63.

4. Miller, *Living Systems*, 39.

5. Jessie L. Miller, "The timer," *Behavioral Science* 35 (1990): 164–96.

Chapter 3

Managing Motivation

As we watch the growth of NewVent and Montero Virtual Realty, we can observe some differences between them. The people at NewVent seem to have a lot of energy and their activity is directed toward getting production on line as quickly as possible. Terry only has to suggest that something needs to be done and someone, or a team, tackles it. Employees are highly focused on the task of building the organization.

At MVR, however, Alex is having difficulty getting the firm moving in the right direction. Alex knows that employees must focus their energies on developing customer awareness of the firm's unique services, and has tried instructing, cajoling, ordering, and offering special incentives, but nothing seems to work. The employees spend much of their time playing with the new technology. The firm is simply waiting, machines brightly polished, for customers to discover it.

DIFFERENCES IN MOTIVATION

Why do some business firms continually strive to expand their markets, whereas others work to consolidate and protect the markets they have? Why does one university emphasize excellence in arts and sciences, whereas another focuses on business and technology? Why does one group of employees seek to improve the quality of its work, whereas another group tries to have fun on the job?

The answer to each of these questions lies in the processes of motivation. These processes determine the direction, intensity, and persistence of behavior. The behavior of an organization, group, or individual is purposeful, not random. By this I mean that behavior is directed at one or more purposes and goals of the system. The intensity and persistence of behavior depend on what is required to meet those purposes and goals. What we observe is not motivation itself but rather the direction, intensity, and persistence of motivated behavior.

Motivation is a basic process of all living systems. Managers often think in terms of motivating individual employees or work groups to perform better. Yet the same process applies to the organization as a whole and to the manager's performance. Alex, for instance, is fascinated by high-tech equipment and has hired people with a similar interest. Job applicants quickly realize that, if they show an interest in the virtual reality technique, Alex becomes more interested in hiring them. Thus, the very first lesson for managers to learn about motivation is

Do not let your desire to motivate others blind you to your own motives and the influences that they are subject to.

The direction of behavior of the organization as a whole, and of each of its components, depends on the template or charter and the decider subsystem of the organization. These are the sources of purposes and goals toward which organizational behavior is directed. To act properly as components of the organization, individual members and groups must be guided by motives that are based on the organization's purposes and goals. In order to get MVR back on track, Alex must reorient the employees to the firm's mission of *using* the virtual reality equipment to help clients find a new home.

Motivation is essential to survival and growth of any living system. It is the connecting link between the needs of the system and their fulfillment. Motivation "drives" or "draws" the system to act on its environment in such a way that required resources are obtained, excess resources and wastes are ejected, and the environment becomes or remains salubrious.

Although a system's behavior may be observable, the motivation that lies behind it is usually hidden within the "black box" of the system. When we speak of human motivation, for instance, we are theorizing about the unobservable sources of a person's behavior. With groups and organizations, on the other hand, it is sometimes possible to peer into the black box and observe at least some of the processes of motivation.

The instructions supplied by the charter of an organization are more accessible than those contained within human genes, although the secrets of the genes are rapidly being uncovered. Group decision processes are more visible than individual decision processes. Even the purposes and goals that guide decisions are typically more overt in organizations than in individuals. Thus, living systems theory offers us an opportunity to learn more about motivation in people by observing the processes of motivation in organizations.

Although motivation occurs whether or not it is understood, knowledge of how motivation works should certainly aid managers in directing the affairs of an organization. This chapter presents models of motivation processes and illustrates them with examples from individual and organizational behavior. The models are based on living systems theory and, therefore, are equally applicable to individuals, groups, and organizations. After presenting the models, we will explore their practical implications. Let us now begin to open a window into the black box of motivation.

TWO BASIC PROCESSES OF MOTIVATION

I have suggested that motivation involves direction by the system's template and/or its decider subsystem. In most cases, both the template and the decider are involved, but it is worthwhile considering template-directed motivation as distinct from that which is decider-directed.

Template-Directed Motivation

As we noted in Chapter 1, the template is the genetic input and/or memetic charter of a living system. It is "the original information input that is the program for [the system's] later structure and process, which can be modified by later matter-energy or information inputs from its environment.[1] The template provides the primal set of directions for the system.

When a system's behavior is directed by its template, no choice is involved. The system *must* act as it does. Such behavior at the organism level is often called instinctive. An animal in heat must seek a mate. A bird must sit on its newly laid eggs. A dog must salivate at the aroma of meat. A flower must open when certain conditions of temperature and moisture exist. A person's epiglottis must close to prevent solids from entering the lungs. Such behavior is built into the regular processes of the organism; it is not learned.

Template-directed behavior is not always raw instinct, however. It may become subject to conscious control and may be modified by learning processes, as indicated in the quoted definition. For example, human adults learn to control their sexual urges and channel them into socially acceptable behavior, even though the sexual urges themselves are instinctive. A business firm's primal mandate to make a profit may be modified by ethical and legal considerations. A nation's basic urge to protect itself may be channeled into a willingness to engage in free trade in order to improve its economy.

Reflexes. Template-directed behavior may be simple or relatively complex. In organisms, simple responses called unconditioned reflexes have been studied extensively by reinforcement theorists. Examples of human unconditioned reflexes include salivation, perspiration, eye blink, and knee jerk. Following Pavlov's classical experiment with a salivating dog, considerable research has been conducted to show how complex conditioned responses can be learned from unconditioned reflexes. Indeed, Skinner asserted that all behavior may be derived in this way.[2] For instance, language may be developed by encouraging infants whenever they make sounds that approximate words.

Drives. Drive theorists have postulated that certain complex patterns of human behavior are essentially innate or template directed. Murray, for instance, published a list of twenty human drives, examples of which are shown in Table 3-1.[3]

Table 3-1
A Sample of Drives as Listed by Murray

Drive	Brief Definition
n Achievement	To accomplish something difficult. To master, manipulate, or organize physical objects, human beings, or ideas. To do this as rapidly and as independently as possible. To overcome obstacles and attain a high standard. To excel oneself. To rival and surpass others. To increase self-regard by the successful exercise of talent.
n Affiliation	To draw near and enjoyably cooperate and reciprocate with an allied other (an other who resembles the subject or who likes the subject). To please and win affection of a cathected object. To adhere and remain loyal to a friend.
n Aggression	To overcome opposition forcefully. To fight. To revenge an injury. To attack, injure, or kill an other. To oppose forcefully or punish an other.
n Defendance	To defend the self against assault, criticism, or blame. To conceal or justify a misdeed, failure, or humiliation. To vindicate the ego.
n Dominance	To control one's human environment. To influence or direct the behavior of an other by suggestion, seduction, persuasion, or command. To dissuade, restrain, or prohibit.

Source: Excerpted from C. S. Hall and G. Lindsey, *Theories in Personality* (New York: Wiley, 1957), 173–74.

Whether human behavior such as aggression and dominance is innate or learned is a matter of controversy. We seldom observe such behavior in its pure, template-directed form. Children quickly learn to modify their aggressive tendencies, for instance. Thus, the expression of aggression may be inhibited, controlled in intensity, transformed into competition, and otherwise modified by learning. Whether there is an innate, template-directed core to this behavior remains an open question.

Although the connection between the template and behavior is hidden within organisms, it can be broken down and analyzed to some extent. We may, of course, observe the direction, intensity, and persistence of the behavior generated by a reflex or drive. We may also observe the consistency of that behavior, and test whether and to what degree it can be modified by learning processes.

Needs. We may also assume that instinctive behavior is purposeful and may speculate about the purposes it serves. Purposes, in living systems theory, are preferred steady state values for system variables.[4] Need (i.e., lack or excess of a resource) is measured in accordance with purpose, as shown in Figure 3-1.[5] That is, the strength of a need is related to the degree of deviation of a variable from its purpose value.

Figure 3-1
The Need Continuum

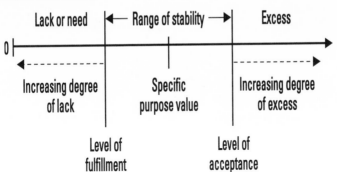

Source: Lane Tracy, "Toward an improved need theory: In response to legitimate criticism," *Behavioral Science* 31 (1986): 211.

Let us apply Figure 3-1 to human needs. Each of us has preferred steady state values for such variables as body temperature, amount of oxygen in the blood, and fullness of the stomach. These values are basically innate, although they may be modified by learning. For instance, while dieting we may learn to tolerate hunger pangs for a longer period.

Surrounding these purpose values is a range of stability within which we hardly notice any lack or excess. Beyond that range, however, we may begin to notice the deviation from the preferred state. We may feel too cool or too warm, a little lethargic or euphoric, hungry or satiated. Or we may notice nothing, but our body may respond by perspiring, becoming sleepy, or moving sluggishly. Whether or not we are consciously aware of the deviation of a variable from its range of stability, the deviation represents a need that may lead to behavior to correct the excess or deficiency.

Excesses are often overlooked as a source of motivation. We tend to think of need in terms of lack. Yet any open system has as much need to get rid of things as to acquire them. We must relieve ourselves of waste products or they will poison us. We must seek employment for our excess energy and skill. We feel an urge to tell others what we know.

Managers must not overlook excesses as sources of motivation.

Living systems have a great variety of needs. At any given moment, some needs are fulfilled (i.e., within the range of stability) and others are active (i.e., there is a lack or excess). It is the active needs that have the potential to motivate behavior.

Managers should try to find out which needs are active within their subor-dinates and in the department and organization as a whole. The behavior of these systems tends to be directed at fulfillment of those needs.

There have been many attempts to enumerate and classify basic human needs.[6] When needs are known, it is often possible to link them to observed behavior. For instance, if we observe a person perspiring under certain conditions of heat, humidity, exertion, or anxiety, we may hypothesize that this instinctive behavior is directed by a need to reduce body temperature to the preferred value. We may even be able to trace the connections through the person's nervous system. Nevertheless, many human needs are unknown or unproven, and the connection of specific behavior to one or more needs is often unclear.

Even less known are the needs of organizations. Perhaps this is because organizations are so heterogeneous. It may be assumed that a business firm has no basic needs in common with a government agency, or that a manufacturing firm shares few needs with a bank.

I believe this assumption is incorrect and that a list of basic needs of organizations could be compiled. For example, it would seem that all organizations require members who are loyal and skilled. A set of customers or clients for the organization's products or services may also be a requirement. Although social organizations might seem to be an exception, the members of such organizations are also the clients.

If we limit ourselves to a subclass of organizations such as business firms, it should be possible to compile a much longer list of basic needs. The work of economists, marketing and human resource specialists, financial analysts, and logistics experts would presumably contribute to such a list. I know of no attempt to compile a list of basic needs of business firms, but you might want to give it a try. More important, *managers will find it useful to make a list of the needs of their own firm.*

Template direction in organizations. Do organizations display instinctive behavior? Let us consider several possible examples. Many corporate charters contain specifications for a board of directors of a certain size and composition. The bylaws may further specify when and how new board members are chosen. When the term of a board member expires or the member dies, the procedures for replacing that board member are automatically invoked. There is no debate about whether or how the board member should be replaced. The behavior is template directed.

Most organizations cannot tolerate internal dishonesty or lack of loyalty. When a member is found to be stealing from the organization or selling its secrets to competitors, expulsion is automatic. Although the written charter and bylaws of the organization may contain no explicit provisions regarding thievery or expulsion, there are likely to be specifications for due process. Definitions of unacceptable member behavior and its consequences may be part of an unwritten charter. Expulsion of the thief is expected not only by the continuing members, but also by the thief. If leaders of the organization attempted to protect and retain the thief, they would risk expulsion themselves. This seems very much like instinctive organizational behavior.

Centralization of authority in times of danger seems to be an automatic response of groups, organizations, communities, and societies. There is a tendency to rally around the leader and to accept the leader's orders when the system is being attacked. This is not necessarily a rational choice—indeed, arguments can be made for the effectiveness of decentralizing certain decisions during a crisis—but the choice does seem to be directed toward basic purposes of the system. It generates a more efficient (although not necessarily more effective) flow of information, concentrates resources at the point of attack, and gives the members or components a feeling of unity of purpose. A leader who failed to take up the reins and provide direction during a crisis would likely be replaced.

Universities tend instinctively to protect free speech. Freedom to inquire after truth and to propagate one's findings are basic to the nature of a university, and may be specified in its charter. Thus, universities as organizations, as well as individual scholars, react automatically to any attempt to stifle different views. Here we encounter a conflict between instinctive behaviors, however. When one person's free speech threatens another's freedom or the continued existence of the university, then the template-directed reaction must be tempered by decisions as to what is the greater danger.

Examining these instances of apparently instinctive behavior in organizations, we find that certain processes are visible. The template of the organization, often in writing, specifies purposes and goals as well as structures and procedures for attaining them. It may even establish a range of stability, as when an organization's policies and procedures specify acceptable salary ranges, return-on-investment guidelines, time limits for responding to grievances, terms of office, and the like. When a deviation from a purpose value occurs, the procedures are automatically invoked and the structures are activated to correct the deviation.

Template-directed behavior requires no decisions and may override any decider-directed behavior that is already occurring. Only when the dictates of the template generate conflict is a decision required. After the deviation is corrected, normal decider-directed behavior resumes.

Figure 3-2
Model of Template-Directed Motivation

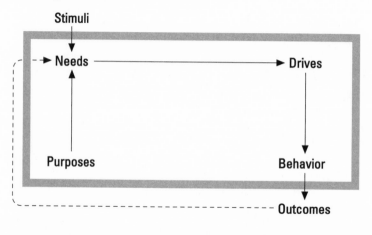

Source: Lane Tracy, "Design for organizational health," *Journal of Business Research* no.12 (1992): 41. Used by permission of the Research Institute Administration Office, College of Economics, Nihon University, Tokyo, Japan.

Model. Figure 3-2 is a model of template-directed motivation. Stimuli, including feedback from outcomes, create a need by moving a variable outside of its range of stability. For instance, cancellation of a customer's order or information indicating excessive inventory may cause the supply of a specific raw material to exceed the upper limits of its purpose. The need to bring this variable back into line triggers a drive that defines and energizes specific behavior, such as cancellation of an order to purchase more of the raw material. This may be an automatic process already programmed into a computer or established by standard operating procedures.

As presented, the model is *homeostatic*, meaning that system variables tend to return to their original values when disturbed. Nevertheless, we should recognize that purposes and goals, even those specified by the template, are subject to change over time. The template, itself, may stipulate change as the system matures. Specifications for the size of the board of directors, the capitalization of the firm, due process, even basic purposes of the organization may be rewritten. Thus, homeostasis becomes a dynamic process as purposes and goals change.

Decider-Directed Motivation

When the decider subsystem is involved, motivation becomes a more complex process. Although purposes and goals may be clear, the behavior required to attain them is no longer predetermined. The system may have to choose among many possible acts that would fulfill a need. It may also not be certain whether, and to what extent, a given act will fulfill a given need. At any moment there will be many competing needs. We do not have the luxury of shutting off the clamor of other needs and considering our needs one at a time. If we are lucky or resourceful, however, we may be able to find ways to fulfill several needs at one time with the same choice of behavior.

To choose among competing needs, the hierarchy of purposes must be invoked as a criterion. Otherwise, the choice of behavior would be random and not purposeful. The decider must choose from competing acts directed at competing purposes. If the choice is to be efficient and effective, some sort of optimization must take place. The survivors, when push comes to shove, are those systems that can fulfill the greatest needs with the least expenditure of resources.

Feedback is required, both to indicate when a need has been met and to allow learning to occur. Only through a learning process can the system improve the effectiveness of its decision making.

Model. Figure 3-3 is a model of decider-directed motivation. It is derived from a combination of various need-based theories of motivation, Vroom's expectancy theory, Locke's goal-setting theory, reinforcement theory, and social learning theory.[7]

To understand the model, let us take a brief guided tour through it. As with the template-directed model, motivation begins with purposes. Purposes (1) generate goals and (2) serve as the baseline for determining needs. Stimuli, such as change in the environment, as well as internal pro-

Figure 3-3
Model of Decider-Directed Motivation

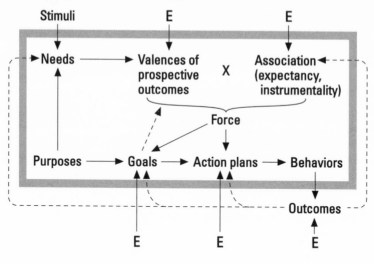

Causal relationship: ⟶
Feedback: ------►
Boundary of system: ▨
External influence: E ⟶

Source: Lane Tracy, "Design for organizational health," *Journal of Business Research* no.12 (1992): 41. Used by permission of the Research Institute Administration Office, College of Economics, Nihon University, Tokyo, Japan.

cesses of consumption and production, generate *strain* in the system, increasing the intensity of certain needs.

Needs are evaluated in terms of intensity and intrinsic importance within a hierarchy of needs (not seen in the model). This hierarchy changes rapidly as new needs are generated and existing ones are fulfilled or lessened. That is, the system constantly maintains a register of the status of all its important variables. The quality of the system's decisions is greatly affected by how complete and up to date this register is. For example, a business manager trying to make decisions on the basis of month-old accounting data would be at a considerable disadvantage compared to one who had computer access to current data.

Returning to the model, various acts that have potential to fulfill one or more needs are constantly being evaluated by the decider. These acts may be drawn from memory or newly synthesized. The decider tries to match acts to needs and assess the likelihood that a given act will fulfill a given need. The *force of motivation* toward a given act is the sum of the products of (1) the *valences* of prospective outcomes of the act (i.e., the estimated worth of these outcomes in terms of need fulfillment) and (2) the *associations* between the act and outcomes (i.e., the likelihood that the act will lead to each outcome).[8]

Force may be calculated for a variety of options, including continuation of current behavior. Each option consists of a set of action plans and goals.

The greater the importance of the decision, the more options should be considered. A rational decider chooses the set that has the greatest force.

Feedback. Behavior results from implementing the chosen action plan. Behavior leads to actual outcomes. Information from outcomes is fed back to various stages of the motivation process. Feedback from these outcomes indicates

1. to what degree needs are fulfilled, thereby changing the estimated worth of those outcomes;
2. to what degree goals have been met;
3. whether acts have been carried out as planned; and
4. to what degree actual outcomes matched expected outcomes.

Feedback of types 1–3 is negative feedback that acts to control behavior and prevent it from persisting beyond its usefulness. When needs are fulfilled and goals are met, the force of the chosen behavior is reduced and the force of other behavior becomes relatively greater. Feedback to the action plan allows the system to modify behavior when it is not proceeding according to plan.

Feedback of type 4, on the other hand, may be positive or negative. When behavior leads to the expected outcome, for instance, this tends to reinforce the association and add force to the chosen behavior. Failure to attain the expected outcome, on the other hand, will lower the association and reduce the force of that behavior. Reinforcement theory is represented by this type of feedback.

Decision making. It is apparent from this model that motivation is tied to decision making. The same force that determines the choice of behavior also motivates that behavior. This has led some theorists and researchers to believe that greater force leads to greater effort.[9] Effort, however, is one of the parameters of each option that is evaluated. To give a simplified example, the decider may choose among three options: work with minimal effort, work with moderate effort, or work with maximum effort. Each option has its own valences, including the valence of the effort itself, and associations. Working with maximum effort may have too much negative valence associated with the effort, or may have expected outcomes that more than fulfill needs. Thus, it is entirely possible that an option involving less effort will have greater force and will be the rational choice.

The choice of behavior involves several other parameters in addition to level of effort. There is a plan of action which specifies the detailed direction, the starting point, and often the duration or persistence of the behavior. Typically there is also a goal for the behavior. The goal reinforces the overall direction of behavior and may indicate when the behavior is to terminate. There may be contingency plans, as well, that specify change in direction, intensity, or duration if certain circumstances arise.

The importance of current behavior is often overlooked when motivation is considered. Unless current behavior has outlived its usefulness by fulfilling all of the needs toward which it was directed, continuation of that behavior should be considered as one of the options. Indeed, interrupting current behavior to shift toward fulfillment of other needs has a cost that should be considered. Production managers would call this the *setup cost*. Economists would consider it as an *opportunity cost*.

It should also be remembered that many action plans call for recurring behavior, perhaps on a regular, periodic basis. For instance, when a person decides to accept employment in a specific job, the decision entails a commitment to show up for work on a regular schedule for an indefinite period of time. Temporarily setting aside that commitment in order to do something else—for example, staying home because of illness—involves a very complex weighing of options against the simple choice of continuing under the current plan.

External influence. Motivation may be influenced externally at several points, indicated by E→ in Figure 3-3. Managers who wish to motivate others in particular directions should take note of these influence points. Let us enumerate and illustrate them.

1. *Stimuli may be manipulated to increase or decrease needs.* For example, a worker might be forbidden to rest until she completes a task, thereby stimulating fatigue as a motive; a child might be guided away from disruptive classroom behavior by fulfilling his need for attention. At the organizational level, payment might be withheld until all conditions of a contract have been met, thereby increasing the contractor's need for money; a firm might dissuade a competitor from invading its market by promising not to invade the competitor's market, thereby decreasing the competitor's need for security.

2. *Valences of prospective outcomes may be increased or decreased.* This may be accomplished by persuasion or by alteration of the worth or cost of those outcomes. An individual may be persuaded that a task will not require as much effort as she thought, or it may actually be made easier by the installation of better machinery. An organization may be persuaded that good performance on a contract is important to its future reputation; payment schedules may be accelerated for good performance or delayed for poor performance.

3. *Associations between behavior and outcomes may be altered.* An association may be strengthened through persuasion or commitments, for instance. A supervisor may encourage a worker to believe that, if he tries hard, he will succeed in the task. The supervisor may also promise that success will lead to a promotion, thereby reducing uncertainty about the link between primary and secondary outcomes. A business firm may convince a competitor that violating a patent will result in a lawsuit; it may file suit on a different matter to demonstrate its willingness to sue.

4. *Goals may be changed.* An individual may be persuaded to set a higher goal for herself, or to accept one that is set for her. An organization may be induced to target a larger market share or reduced costs. Setting a higher goal tends to increase the valence of the outcomes associated with that goal (as indicated by a dashed arrow in Figure 3-3) and may also influence action plans.

5. *Action plans may be altered directly.* An employee may be taught a better way to do his job. An organization may discover improved methods or better materials that call for different behavior.

6. *Actual outcomes may be changed.* If this is done before the act is chosen, it may influence the choice. Otherwise, it affects feedback and may influence future choices or the persistence of the current choice. An announced pay increase may induce better performance during the pay period; an unexpected bonus may induce better performance in the next period—but only if a connection is perceived between pay and performance. A firm may offer a larger order in exchange for a lower price, or may cut the size of its order in response to a price increase.

The foregoing analysis of influence points suggests the following advice to managers:

> When attempting to change an employee's behavior through influence at any of these six points, a manager should keep in mind that the employee's current behavior is also motivated. Thus, influence should be directed not only at increasing the force toward the desired behavior, but also at decreasing the force behind the current behavior.[10]

MOTIVATIONAL INTERACTION

The existence of these six points of external influence on motivation leads us to another important point:

> Motivation almost always involves interaction between two or more living systems; they motivate each other.

Motivation comes from within the system, but it is constantly responding to external forces. Furthermore, the influences are reciprocal rather than unilateral.

Examples of reciprocal motivation abound. Children influence the motivation of parents; by "being good" a boy motivates his mother to give him candy. Workers influence the motivation of supervisors; by acting collectively they may motivate the supervisor to go easy on discipline. Business firms influence the motivation of the government; by lobbying intensively they may motivate legislators to pass favorable laws. In each case, however, there is obviously reciprocal influence at work. The parent induces good behavior in the child, the supervisor obtains cooperation from the workers, and the legislators gain campaign contributions from business firms.

Figure 3-4 presents a model of motivational interaction between two living systems. The model is constructed by unfolding and connecting two models of individual motivation (Figure 3-3) at their points of influence.

Obviously, the possible lines of influence are very complex. Because of this complexity, the influence of one system on the motivation, and thereby the behavior, of another system is very difficult to predict. This complexity is compounded by the fact that, at any given moment, a living system may be interacting with many other systems. For example, an employee interacts with the organization as a whole, with her work group, with her supervisor, and with individual fellow workers. In the background, there are also interactions with family and community. The employee must weigh all of these influences in choosing her course of action.

There is similar complexity at the organizational level of motivation. The action plans and goals chosen by a business firm are influenced by many competitors, suppliers, and customers, as well as by government regulation, public opinion, and the behavior of employees both individually and collectively.

Managers may seek to dominate and influence the choices that other people make, but they cannot avoid being influenced themselves.

PRACTICAL CONSIDERATIONS

Living systems theory leads us to the conclusion that motivation is a much more complex process than often pictured. Need theories only scratch the surface, expectancy theory is too simplistic, goal-setting theory focuses on one small aspect of influence, reinforcement theory refuses to look within the black box. These theories may each be useful in certain

Figure 3-4
Model of Motivational Interaction between Systems

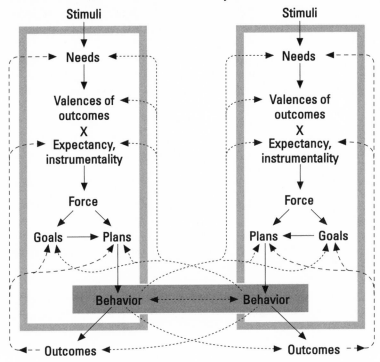

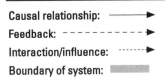

Source: Lane Tracy, "Motivational interaction between living systems," *Systems Practice* 2 (1989): 338.

circumstances, but they often fail because they leave out important processes, feedback loops, and/or sources of external influence.

Interactive Motivation

The first lesson we may learn, therefore, is

Be wary of simplistic, unilateral approaches to motivation.

Motivation is like a chess game. A player who always attacks and ignores defense will usually lose, as will one who always plays defense and never tries to attack. The wise player is aware of both the influence his moves have on his opponent and the influence his opponent's moves have on himself.

Chief executive officers and boards of directors, who serve as the top-echelon deciders for organizations, must likewise be aware of the complex interactions that influence the motivation of organizations. To fulfill its own needs for profit, market share, innovation, efficiency, and so forth, an organization must also fulfill needs of its employees, shareholders, creditors, customers, suppliers, and the government.

As organizations become larger and more powerful, it is all too easy to forget or ignore the motivations of these other systems. That is why successful business firms often find themselves suddenly confronted with a militant work force, restrictive regulations, or new competition. To avoid such unpleasant surprises

Executives must continue to be aware of the interests of the many other systems with which they interact.

Awareness and understanding of organizational needs begin at home. Many organizations, particularly young ones, have little knowledge of their requirements for survival and growth. Undercapitalization is a frequent cause of the demise of new businesses. Another major lack in many business firms is accurate, up-to-date information about internal processes and/or the environment. This lack is often coupled with inadequate information-processing subsystems.

A warning signal that a chronic lack exists is the fact that managers are constantly motivated to try to relieve that lack. If managers spend most of their time trying to find out what is going on, for instance, then it is time to make changes in the flow of information. Thus:

Managers should be aware of their own needs and the needs of the organization.

Goal Setting

Organizational goals are much more apt to be stated formally than individual goals. Yet the motivational effects of goal setting have been studied only as a phenomenon of individuals. The model in Figure 3-3 indicates that setting a high goal increases the valence of that outcome by linking the goal to the system's self-concept, thereby adding force to the chosen behavior. Does this also occur in organizations? Do organizations that set realistic but high specific goals for themselves perform better than those that do not set goals, or that set vague, general goals? I suspect that goal setting works for groups and organizations just as it does for individuals, but this is a question worthy of investigation.

Points of Influence

There are many points at which a manager may attempt to influence the motivation, and thus the behavior, of employees. This chapter has indicated that a manager may influence employees' motivation by

1. *stimulating needs that can be fulfilled by the desired behavior;*
2. *increasing the perceived worth of prospective outcomes;*
3. *strengthening the perceived link between behavior and outcomes;*
4. *setting or encouraging employees to set higher, more specific goals;*
5. *teaching better ways to do the job;* and
6. *increasing the rewards associated with the outcome.*

Feedback

Feedback is a very important part of the motivation model. Perceptions of the outcomes of behavior, for instance, depend on the quality and timeliness of feedback from those outcomes. From this we may conclude that

Managers should pay close attention to feedback as a motivational tool. Feedback can be used to support continuation of desired behavior and cessation of undesirable behavior.

Many firms have discovered the importance of feedback at the individual and group levels. Pay works as a motivator when it is linked to specific performance indicators.[11] Work quality improves when operators inspect their own work, because they receive immediate feedback about quality. Safety campaigns are effective when they provide work groups with regularly updated information about their safety record. In each of these cases, feedback works positively to strengthen the association between behavior and the desired outcome.

There is also a negative effect of feedback to the extent that the need (for pay, quality, safety, etc.) is fulfilled. Yet each of these needs is constantly being renewed by other stimuli. A more valuable form of negative feedback is to the action plan. If a given set of planned actions is not attaining the desired quality standard, for instance, the operator can modify the plan.

How does feedback work at the organization level? That depends on what kinds of information top management is receiving about performance. In many firms, the CEO looks only at financial data. Feedback is provided on cash flow, variances from budget, cost savings, stock price, and other financial indicators. This allows control of, and provides increased motivation toward, the behaviors that generate the indicated outcomes. However, such limited feedback tends to lose sight of the effects of the chosen behavior on market share, consumer preference, new-product development, product quality, employee morale, and the long-term health of the organization.

Feedback in the organization is too important to be left to chance. Top management must ensure that it is not flying blind. Therefore:

Develop a broad set of indicators that provide feedback with respect to all of the major purposes of the organization.

If product quality, employee morale, cost reduction, new-product development, market share, and profits are each important interests of the organization, then top management should receive regular feedback about all of those variables.

Several new approaches to measurement of organizational processes show promise of providing better feedback to managers. Swanson has attempted to develop means for extracting more accurate information about the state of a living organization from its accounting data.[12] A survey approach called living systems process analysis has been developed to assess performance of critical subsystems.[13] Total quality management (TQM) collects and feeds back a variety of statistical measurements that enable employees to improve work processes.[14]

Decision Making

Except for instinctual behavior, motivation is inherently linked to decision making. The models presented in this chapter show that the same processes that generate decisions also produce the motivation to carry out those decisions. Thus:

Anything that improves decisions within the organization is likely also to improve motivation in desired directions.

The key to good organizational decision making is direction. Are decisions being made in the best interests of the organization? To answer that question, we (and the organization's members) must have a clear idea of what those "best interests" are. Do operators understand the desired balance between quality and quantity of output? Does the R&D department understand the interests of the organization with respect to basic research versus product development? Is the marketing department aware of the desired balance between sustaining existing markets and developing new ones? Does top management understand the relative needs of the organization for long-term growth and short-term profit maximization?

To make good decisions, employees must understand the interests of the organization.

Purposes and Goals

The first stage of the decision-making process is to establish purposes and goals toward which the decision is directed.[15] These purposes and goals may already be established by prior decisions or the template but, whatever the source, they must be there to guide the current decision. Purposes and goals guide the direction of the chosen behavior as well as its intensity and persistence. A clear conception of purposes and goals is essential to proper motivation in an organization. Ergo:

Managers can go far toward improving motivation within an organization by clarifying and communicating the purposes and goals of the organization.

Everyone who makes decisions for the organization, and that generally includes all members to some extent, must have this clear understanding of purposes and goals. Machine operators and clerks, if they are to be well motivated, must know the purposes of their work and the goals they are seeking to attain. Even a general understanding of the overall purposes and goals of the organization is helpful. A sales clerk should know, for instance, whether good service and customer satisfaction is more or less important than adherence to rules.

A basic task of management is to communicate the purposes and goals of the organization to all members. Peters and Waterman found that one of the characteristics of excellent organizations is that the leader(s) have a vision of what the organization can accomplish, and they communicate this vision to employees.[16] In doing so they may make extensive use of the devices of corporate culture: rites and ceremonies, stories, symbols, and special language.[17] A well-formed and fully communicated culture helps to provide all deciders with an understanding of the purposes and goals of the organization, and hence motivates them in proper directions. The models of motivation presented in this chapter help us to understand why this is so.

NOTES

1. James G. Miller, *Living Systems* (New York: McGraw-Hill, 1978), 34.

2. B. F. Skinner, *The Behavior of Organisms: An Experimental Analysis* (New York: Appleton-Century Crofts, 1938).

3. Henry A. Murray, *Explorations in Personality* (New York: Oxford, 1938).

4. Miller, *Living Systems*, 39.

5. Lane Tracy, *The Living Organization: Systems of Behavior* (New York: Praeger, 1989), 62.

6. Abraham H. Maslow, "A theory of human motivation," *Psychological Review* 50 (1943): 370–96; Clayton P. Alderfer, *Existence, Relatedness, and Growth: Human Needs in Organizational Settings* (New York: Free Press, 1972); Lane Tracy, "Toward an improved need theory: In response to legitimate criticism," *Behavioral Science* 31 (1986): 205–18.

7. Edwin A. Locke, "Toward a theory of task motivation and incentives," *Organizational Behavior and Human Performance* 3 (1968): 594–601; Victor H. Vroom, *Work and Motivation* (New York: McGraw-Hill, 1964); Gerald R. Salancik and Jeffrey Pfeffer, "A social information processing approach to job attitudes and task design," *Administrative Science Quarterly* 23 (1978): 224–53; G. R. Ferris, T. A. Beehr, and D. C. Gilmore, "Social facilitation: A review and alternative conceptual model," *Academy of Management Review* 3 (1978): 338–47.

8. This part of the model is based on expectancy theory. See Vroom, *Work and Motivation*.

9. Jay Galbraith and L. L. Cummings, "An empirical investigation of the motivational determinants of task performance," *Organizational Behavior and Human Performance* 2 (1967): 237–57; George Graen, "Instrumentality theory or work motivation," *Journal of Applied Psychology Monograph* 53 (1969): 1–25.

10. Kurt Lewin, *Field Theory in Social Science* (New York: Harper & Row, 1951).

11. Lyman W. Porter and Edward E. Lawler, III, *Managerial Attitudes and Performance* (Homewood, IL: Richard D. Irwin, 1968).

12. G. A. Swanson and James G. Miller, *Measurement and Interpretation in Accounting: A Living Systems Theory Approach* (Westport, CT: Quorum, 1989); G. A. Swanson and Hugh L. Marsh, *Internal Auditing Theory—A Systems View* (Westport, CT: Quorum, 1991); G. A. Swanson, *Macro Accounting and Modern Money Supplies* (Westport, CT: Quorum, 1993).

13. Stephen L. Merker, "A living systems process analysis of an urban hospital," *Behavioral Science* 32 (1987): 304–14.

14. W. Edwards Deming, *Out of the Crisis* (Cambridge, MA: MIT Center for Advanced Engineering Study, 1982); Mary Walton, *The Deming Management Method* (New York: Putnam, 1986).

15. Miller, *Living Systems*, 68.

16. Thomas J. Peters and Robert H. Waterman, Jr., *In Search of Excellence: Lessons from America's Best-Run Companies* (New York: Harper & Row, 1982).

17. Vijay Sathe, "Implications of corporate culture: A manager's guide to action," *Organizational Dynamics* 12, no. 2 (1983): 5–23.

Chapter 4

Managing Resources and Power

Terry has put together a thriving organization. NewVent is operating efficiently, the employees are highly motivated, and the products are selling like—well, like magnetic flanges. It is time to enlarge operations, but as Terry begins to plan for expansion, problems loom on the horizon.

The first problem is that there is no room for growth at the present location. The current building is filled to capacity, there are no empty buildings nearby, there are no vacant lots on which to build new facilities, and the current structure cannot support upward expansion. If NewVent is to grow, it will have to move all or part of the organization.

Another problem is that Cryorubber, Inc., the current supplier of supercooling hose, says it cannot increase shipments of this essential component until it carries out its own expansion plans. There are no other suppliers in this country.

NewVent will also have to hire and train many new employees. Terry is particularly worried about the availability of cryogenic engineers. To expand the product line, NewVent will need their expertise, but good ones are hard to find. In addition, some of the current employees will have to be retrained.

Finally, money may be a problem. NewVent's current budget is barely adequate to support the current level of business. It is obvious that the firm is going to need a lot more capital to finance the expansion. Yet, Uni-Globe is in a recessionary mood and reluctant to put up the money for growth.

Each of these problems has to do with the availability of resources. Living systems require regular inputs of a variety of resources in order to survive. Growth requires even greater inputs. Just as you need air, water, food, warmth, and information about your surroundings, so a business firm requires inputs of raw materials, energy, machinery, people (as employees and customers), money, and information about the economy, new processes, and so on. Planning the acquisition of such resources is a major part of management.

TYPES OF RESOURCES

A *resource* is anything that is capable of satisfying a need of a living system.[1] Needs and need fulfillment were defined in Chapter 3 as applying to all levels of living systems. Thus, if NewVent has a need for 900 meters of supercooling hose per day in order to maintain current production rates, a resource for NewVent would be anything that can meet that need. When only the hose made by Cryorubber can do the job, then the need is very specific. Other types of hose would become resources for NewVent if they could be substituted for the Cryorubber product.

When a living system does not have enough of a resource, or the rate of inflow is inadequate, we say that the system has a need or lack. When the system has too much of a resource, even though it may be needed in some amount, we say that the system has an excess. If other systems require the same resource and have a lack of it, the first system may be able to sell or trade its excess for something it needs. Otherwise, it will have to expel the excess as waste. In either case, resources must sometimes be output as well as input.

Resources come in three basic forms: matter, energy, and information. As we noted in Chapter 1, living systems have a set of critical subsystems to process matter-energy and another set to process information. Specifically with respect to inputs, for instance, the ingestor takes in matter-energy and the input transducer receives information. But we also found that information is carried by markers of matter or energy. Thus, processing resource inputs often involves both the ingestor and the input transducer. For instance, receiving a letter requires processing both the paper (e.g., opening and filing) and the message (e.g., reading and understanding).

Matter

Inputs of matter into NewVent include both material that is consumed and material that is transformed for export from the system. Machinery is intended for consumption, albeit slowly, as acknowledged by the accounting procedure of depreciation. Inputs such as coal, natural gas, and air (i.e., oxygen) are consumed by converting them into heat and other forms of energy. Food is brought in by employees and eaten on the premises.

Inputs of raw materials and subassemblies, on the other hand, are generally not consumed by the system. Rather, they are transformed by the converter and producer processes and eventually expelled as products and wastes. The products will be consumed by another system. Wastes, including scrap, rejected products, used paper, expended machinery, and polluted air and water, generally have no market but nevertheless must be eliminated from the system. NewVent may have to pay other systems to remove some of these wastes.

Management must plan for the acquisition of material resources, marketing of products, and removal of wastes.

Because expended and transformed matter is constantly being expelled from the system, it must be replaced or the system will quickly shrink to nothing. On the other hand, failure to move products out the door or get rid of wastes would rapidly bloat the system and clog the storage and distributor processes.

Energy

NewVent receives free heat and light from the sun, but must supplement these sources by purchasing electric power. Thus, some energy production is dispersed to an electric utility. The utility may harvest "free" energy from water, wind, nuclear, and geothermal sources, or produce it by burning coal, oil, or natural gas. NewVent also employs conversion processes to generate energy, burning natural gas to heat the building and gasoline to propel its fleet of cars and trucks.

Energy acquisition is as important as maintaining the input of materials. Fortunately, however, in an industrially developed society energy is relatively easy to obtain. You simply have to make sure that you can afford to pay for it. Except for energy-producing systems, energy also poses fewer problems with respect to storage and disposal. A consumer of electric power, for instance, can generally obtain the power on a just-in-time basis. With good planning and efficient use there may only be a small amount of waste heat to get rid of. The rest of the energy goes into the product and is sold for profit.

Information

Information tends to be overlooked as an important input, because it lacks substance, its worth is often fleeting, and it may appear to be free.

(We also tend to disregard free matter-energy such as air and sunlight.) However, a manufacturing firm such as NewVent needs many kinds of information input, and a service firm like Montero Virtual Realty is even more dependent on information.

NewVent requires information from the environment about consumer needs and preferences, availability of materials and labor, competitors' actions, new developments in materials and machinery, new production processes, government regulations, prices and inflation, prospects for future orders, transportation and shipping costs, and the weather. Some of this information can, indeed, be obtained free except for the cost of employees' time in gathering it, whereas other information, such as legal expertise and plans for a new production process, may be purchased at high cost.

Much information has rapidly depreciating worth, because the situation is swiftly changing. For instance, weather forecasts, sales opportunities, and the value of the dollar tend to change daily. Thus:

Managerial planning should focus on assigning tasks and designing procedures for monitoring important sources of information.

NewVent salespeople, for instance, know that it is part of their job to listen to customers, take note of expressed preferences, probe for details, and report the results to someone who is charged with compiling this information and passing it on to the product designers. MVR's employees are instructed to be on the lookout for new listings.

Two types of organizational resources—people and money—deserve special treatment, even though they fall within the three categories above. In his modeling of industrial dynamics, Forrester found it useful to differentiate flows of people and money from flows of other matter, energy, and information.[2] Organizations typically dedicate specific departments (e.g., finance and human resources) to the acquisition of these special resources.

People

People are sources of both energy and information. When you hire someone into a firm, you expect them to satisfy needs for both labor and expertise or skill. Furthermore, people are renewable resources. They report to work each day with renewed energy, and they are capable of acquiring new skills and gaining new expertise. Organizations do not usually consume people as they use up energy and raw materials. Like markers that hold information, people are carriers of resources, rather than being the resource themselves.

One peculiarity of people as resources is that, absent the institution of slavery, the organization cannot own them. A business firm only rents or leases the skills and effort of its employees. The organization may try to obtain a longer-term commitment from employees in various ways, such as employment contracts, employee stock option programs (ESOPs), and retirement benefits, but the degree of "ownership" is limited. For this reason, as we will see, human resources require more maintenance than most other kinds of resources.

Money

Money is also a carrier of resources. It is a particular kind of marker for information about worth. Money represents purchasing power, the ability to acquire a variety of other resources. We do not consume money, we exchange it. Money may also represent debt, showing that we owe certain outputs to other systems.

Money comes in a variety of forms. Metal coins and paper bills are common forms, but beads or cows also serve as money in some cultures. Money is represented indirectly by bonds and stocks, so long as there is a ready market for them. Paper checks and plastic credit cards are markers for money.

Increasingly, money is conveyed by electronic markers. Paychecks are deposited directly to the bank and bills are paid by computer. Bonds and stocks are traded electronically. Any kind of marker can be used for money, so long as it is generally accepted as such. As I write this, the State of California is paying its employees with IOUs and the banks in that state are accepting them as money.

The important thing about money is not the form of the marker, but the fact that there is general agreement about the amount of worth it represents. Problems occur when that agreement breaks down; that is, when banks no longer accept California's IOUs, or your checks bounce, or the worth of the Russian ruble declines rapidly in world markets.

Problems also occur when there is disagreement about accessibility of money. Money that is tied up in obligations or is deposited in a failed bank may exist on paper, but it is not available for trade. Accounts receivable represent money that is owed you, that can be calculated as part of your assets, but you can't spend it yet.

One of the generally desirable features of money is its storability. Money is much easier to store than raw materials, finished goods, electric energy, or personal service. Thus, money is used to hold worth or purchasing power until it is needed.

Because money is held over long periods, conventions have arisen for adjusting the value of money according to changes over time. Money "earns interest" in many circumstances. Other resources, such as property, gold, diamonds, and art, may also increase in value when held over a period of time, but the conventions for revaluation are less certain. Also, the storage costs for many resources exceed any likely increase in worth.

EFFICIENCY AND SURVIVAL

The *efficiency* of a living system is "the ratio of the success of its performance to the costs involved."[3] Success is measured by the degree to which the system attains its purposes and goals. For a business firm this is usually determined by the worth of its outputs and its assets. The costs are the worth of the resources consumed, including matter, energy, information, money, and people's time.

The efficiency of a mechanical system can never be greater than 100 percent. That is, its output cannot have more matter-energy than its input. A living system, on the other hand, measures worth differently. It can and should generate outputs of greater worth than its inputs. The gain is measured in terms of the values of the system.

Increasing efficiency is a major principle behind the success and survival of living systems. In the long run, systems that are able to do more with less will outlast or outreproduce those that make inefficient use of inputs.[4] Thus, managers are constantly looking for less costly means of production.

Increasingly, firms have turned to automation, replacing people with machinery and computers. Even though the initial cost of the machines may be higher than the cost of the people they replace, increased performance may more than compensate. For instance, when automakers switched to automated machining of engine parts, they were suddenly able to produce tolerances finer than those traditionally found in a Rolls-Royce engine.

Yet the current work force can often perform more efficiently, if given the chance. Employees usually are aware of better methods, but their ideas may be ignored. Their efficiency may also be hampered by inferior materials, poorly maintained equipment, and faulty scheduling. In other words, the efficiency of management must also be examined. In a number of cases firms have improved efficiency by eliminating levels of management and training employees to participate in decision making. Managers are needed only where they add value to the product or service.

A concern for reducing costs may easily lead to trouble, if the other side of the efficiency ratio is forgotten. Cost "savings" that lead to inferior performance do not save anything. The Exxon *Valdez* disaster could largely have been prevented if spill-containment crews and equipment had not been axed in a fit of cost cutting.[5]

Managers must pay close attention to costs, but also to results. Efficiency is a combination of the two.

EXCHANGE PROCESSES

Resources are constantly being transformed and exchanged between living systems. Often the exchange of resources is reciprocal. In a complex economy, however, money offers a means of creating reciprocality where it would not otherwise exist. The exchange of resources other than money may then form a long chain of linked systems. Let us look first at direct exchange of nonmonetary resources, and then at chains of exchange.

Dyadic Exchange

The basic "molecule" of living systems is the *dyad*—two systems linked in reciprocal exchange. Examples abound among people and social systems. A married couple exchange love, honor, and respect for each other's desires. A parent gives a child love, protection, sustenance, and knowledge in exchange for love, obedience, and the implied promise of future benefits. Laborers trade their skills and energy to an employer in exchange for meaningful work, job security, tools—and money. Citizens exhange loyalty, taxes, and obedience to the government for security, stability, and maintenance of the infrastructure. A farmer trades part of the crop to a cooperative in exchange for seed and fertilizer. Members of a political party give their time and energy to the party for camaraderie and an opportunity to exert influence on the government. Members of a college football team trade their time, skill, and effort for a scholarship, coaching, and a chance to be part of a winning group.

Figure 4-1
Dyadic Exchange between Employer and Employee

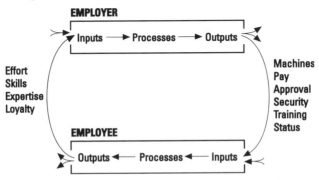

Source: Adapted from L. Tracy, "A dynamic living-systems model of work motivation," *Systems Research* 1, no. 3 (1984): 201.

Figure 4-1 shows the dyadic exchange relationship between NewVent and one of its employees. Note that the two systems in this exchange are not at the same level. One is a person, the other an organization. This is typical of many dyadic exchanges. The only requirement is that both be living systems.

Both parties fulfill a variety of important needs through this particular exchange relationship, and the transactions recur on a regular basis. An exchange could be a unique event based on a single resource flowing in each direction; for instance, holding a door open for a stranger in exchange for a thank you. However, when many resources are traded, or the resources fulfill important needs, or the exchange is repeated frequently or on a regular basis, a strong bond is likely to develop between the systems.

Indeed, the dyad may, itself, become a living system, as in a marriage or a merger of associated business firms. When a dyad develops its own decider subsystem—that is, decisions are made for its sake and on the basis of its values—it becomes a living system in its own right.

Another feature of the dyad that should be observed is the external relationships represented in Figure 4-1 by arrows going nowhere. In fact, these arrows connect to other systems not shown in the figure. These other systems are alternative sources of resources and additional customers for the goods and services of the dyad's members.

Living systems are not the only providers or recipients of resources. Some forms of matter, energy, and information are obtained from the nonliving environment. NewVent receives air, light, heat, gravity, and information about its physical surroundings from inanimate sources. Some outputs, especially wastes, also go to the nonliving environment.

Relationships outside of the dyad provide a means of escape if the dyadic exchange becomes inadequate or unfair to one of the parties. If the exchange between NewVent and the employee becomes unsatisfactory, for instance, the firm can hire other workers and the employee can seek another job. Also, neither is totally dependent on the other, because each requires resources that the other cannot supply. For instance, the firm does not look to the employee for raw materials or financing, and the employee does not expect love or spiritual comfort from the firm.

Dependency

The degree of dependency of one system on another is determined by several factors: the number of different resources exchanged, the importance of those resources to the recipient, the frequency or regularity of the exchange, and the availability of substitutes or alternate sources. An employee is more dependent on a firm that supplies wages, housing, medical benefits, and a retirement plan than on one that offers only wages. We are generally more dependent on physicians than on attorneys, although that depends on what kind of trouble we are in. A firm that offers regular, full-time employment creates a greater dependency than one that hires people for part-time work as needed. NewVent is more dependent on Cryorubber, its only vendor of supercooling hose, than on a firm that supplies nuts and bolts. MVR is dependent on agencies of the network in other cities to supply listings and videodisks.

Dependency in a dyad cuts both ways, but it may not cut equally. An employee may need the job and its benefits more than the firm needs the employee's services. In a medical emergency, we may require the physician's attention more than the physician needs income from additional patients. Cryorubber requires customers like NewVent, but perhaps not as strongly as NewVent needs Cryorubber's product. Inequalities of dependency give one system power over the other, a topic we shall tackle shortly.

The degree of interdependence of systems in a dyad is a measure of the cohesiveness of the bond. It is equal to the lesser of the dependencies of the two systems on each other, because each system owes at least that much to the other.

Degree of interdependence is an important variable for management, indicating, for example, the strength of the bond that ties employees to the firm and the firm to its employees. It also indicates the strength of bonds with customers and suppliers.

Stars and Chains of Exchange

So far, although noting the existence of other relationships, we have focused on dyads. Another way to analyze the relationships and dependencies among living systems is to trace the resource inputs and outputs that support one system.

Taking NewVent as an example, we would need to list every living and nonliving system that contributes inputs, although we might conveniently aggregate some of them, such as employees or suppliers. We would also list all of the systems that receive outputs from NewVent. Following convention, sources of input could be ranged on the left and recipients of nonmonetary output could be placed on the right. Adding arrows representing resource flow, the result would be a star-burst figure such as Figure 4-2.

Additional information could be added to the figure. Arrows could be made fat or thin to represent the importance of the resource, and solid or dashed to show the frequency of exchange. Different-colored arrows could be used to represent matter, energy, information, people, and money.

Figure 4-2
Resource Star

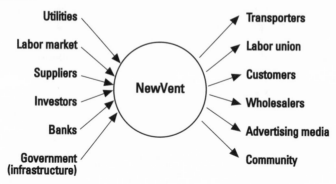

The star, with or without these elaborations, is useful to show the variety and complexity of relationships necessary to support a living system. It becomes obvious from such a figure that no single dyadic relationship can dominate a system's continual search for resources to support life.

Another way of depicting resource exchange is to picture it as a chain of dyadic relationships. We could do this, for instance, to show what happens to a single resource as it flows through a series of systems, or to show how money is used to balance a series of exchanges. Figure 4-3 is an example of the latter usage.

Figure 4-3
Resource Chain

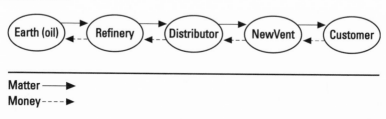

In some cases, the chain may return to its starting point, forming a complete circle. Even then it represents only a small segment of the exchange relationships among the systems involved. Each system in the chain is the center of a star, and many of the systems in each star are interrelated. Chains, stars, and dyads are simplifications that allow us to isolate and examine local areas of a vast complex of relationships between living systems. Managers may find them useful in analyzing the firm's relationships and dependencies.

Economists have attempted to model the whole set of economic exchange relationships in the U.S. economy. Very large sets of equations and complex computer models have been employed for the purpose, but, so far, the results have been disappointing. At this stage dyads, stars, and chains seem to be more useful.

STORING RESOURCES

Living systems do not depend on being able to find resources for input when needed. All living systems possess or have access to matter-energy storage and memory subsystems. These subsystems enable a system to retain resources within its boundary and to access them when needed.

Living systems display a remarkable penchant for increasing their natural storage capacity through use of artifacts. Many animals, either individually or in groups, store food in nests, hives, and similar structures. Human individuals and groups use storage huts, closets, cabinets, shelves, racks, drawers, crawl spaces, attics, garages, refrigerators, freezers, tanks, boxes, suitcases, trunks, batteries, books, tape recorders, cameras, and computer disks—all to store various forms of matter-energy and information.

Organizations are particularly adept at expanding their storage capacity. Manufacturing firms, for instance, devote considerable attention to maintaining inventories of raw materials, work in process, and finished goods, as well as retaining correspondence, production records, orders, billing and payment records, personnel data, and so forth. Some organizations, such as naval ships, must even devise ways to store their members who are not at work.

Entire organizations, such as libraries, museums, warehouses, banks, insurance companies, waste disposal firms, burial associations, and water departments, are devoted primarily to storage. Governments often concern themselves with the storage of natural resources through forest and wildlife preserves, energy reserves, fuel depots, and dams. Armaments are stored in armories, hangars, and bunkers. Government records are retained in archives and computer networks.

People are not stored directly by most organizations. This process is dispersed to the employees, who take responsibility for housing and feeding themselves. But organizations do try to build up and retain human banks of skill and knowledge. Business firms spend billions of dollars annually on training programs for employees. Purposes of these programs include preparing employees for promotion, retraining workers whose skills have become obsolete, cross-training employees so that they will be more versatile, and educating workers in problem-solving skills to improve productivity.

The assumption behind industrial training programs is that people are repositories of valuable knowledge and skill resources, and that these resources can be tapped when needed. Yet employees are free to take their knowledge and skills elsewhere. Thus, firms must also devise means to retain employees.

Periodic wage and salary increases; opportunities for promotion; and forms of compensation based on seniority, such as pensions and vacations, are commonly used to strengthen employees' ties to the firm. Developing loyalty through a sense of identification with the firm is another means. Adhering to a "guaranteed lifetime employment" policy, as many Japanese firms and a few American companies try to do, is one of the strongest means of ensuring that an investment in training will not be lost through employee turnover.

A lifetime employment policy requires careful planning, however. There must be a continuing need for the employees, or the efficiency of the system will suffer. The 1993 recession in Japan created overstaffing problems in many Japanese firms, as well as severe dislocations when a firm went bankrupt. Likewise, the decline of the mainframe computer business forced IBM to lay off employees for the first time in many decades, at a high cost in morale.

The variety of means that living systems have developed and are still developing to increase their storage capacity attests to the importance of memory and matter-energy storage. It is evident that there is competitive advantage, at least up to a point, in being able to store more than other systems. Improving on nature in the matter of storage capacity is a primary focus of survival and competition among living systems.

Efficiency and Storage

How can we reconcile the principle of increasing efficiency with the observation that successful systems devote much of their resources to development of increased storage capacity? Is this an efficient use of resources? If so, how? If not, how do the principles of efficiency and storage capacity interact?

In order to begin to answer these questions we must first understand why matter-energy storage and memory are so critical to the health of living systems. How does storage capacity contribute to the survivability of a living system?

There are circumstances in which no matter-energy storage or memory is necessary. If a system exists in an environment that automatically makes available in sufficient amounts whatever resources the system requires, then there is no need for the system to store anything. Bacteria often experience such an environment, as do human infants. Even so, bacteria and babies possess innate storage capacity for nutrients, water, and certain minerals. Perhaps this capacity is a vestige of harder times, but we must assume it has survival potential.

As the environment becomes less benign or more variable, the need for storage capacity increases. Certain resources may be available on a sporadic basis, for instance. When a living system depletes the resources in its immediate vicinity, as a tribe of hunter-gatherers might, it must store enough to survive during the period of migration to a new place. During the spring, a farmer stores water in a pond for use during the dry summer months. Seeds are stored in the fall for replanting in the spring. These activities require memory of the recurring patterns as well as capacity to hold whatever is needed for the future.

As long as resource deficiencies in the environment are predictable, there is no need for expansion of storage capacity beyond a calculable size. Our built-in capacity to retain air, water, and nutrients probably reflects evolutionary survival calculations as to the maximum length of time we are likely to be deprived of each of these resources.

Business firms are often able to anticipate seasonal variations of supply and demand and can minimize inventory accordingly. When changes in the availability of resources are predictable, the principles of efficiency and sufficiency can be reconciled. It is when change becomes unpredictable that storage capacity emerges as a dominant factor.

Buffers

Management under conditions of uncertainty is a major theme of the literature of business administration. Managers attempt to convert uncertainty or unpredictability into risk, which is manageable. A primary method in this conversion process is the use of buffers.

The technical core functions of an organization are surrounded by buffer departments that protect the core from environmental uncertainty.[6] Furthermore, buffer stocks are used to protect critical functions from experiencing a shortage of any resources they may require. Buffer stocks may exist at each stage of system operation: at the input stage in the form of ready access to information, energy, a line of credit, parts, and raw materials; at the transformation stage as materials inventory and semi-finished assemblies; and at the output stage in the form of finished products inventory.

Buffers require storage capacity. Buffer departments need office space and other resources. A major part of their normal activity consists of gathering and storing information in an attempt to reduce uncertainty. Buffer stocks consisting of materials, semi-finished assemblies, and finished products require storage space. System resources are invested both in storage capacity (i.e., space and memory) and in activities such as research and development that are designed to reduce uncertainty to a manageable level.

Management takes a calculated risk of wasting resources in unnecessary activities and excess capacity, judging that the risk is likely to be less harmful to the system than unanticipated environmental change might be.

Note that buffers may be dispersed to other living systems or the nonliving environment. In using credit, for instance, an individual or organization allows a financial institution to be the actual holder of the buffer stock. Mining and logging firms depend on the land as a repository of their raw materials. Information may be gleaned from libraries, reporting services, customers and competitors, and the physical environment; the system may simply invest in the means of accessing these sources of data. Nevertheless, such sources should be considered adjuncts of a system's storage and memory subsystems, if the system makes regular, planned use of them.

Sometimes a key resource cannot be stored. For instance, Virtual Realty and its affiliate agencies cannot effectively stockpile properties for sale. In such cases, the system may store something else, such as money, to carry it over a slack period.

Risk Management

A general observation is that living systems invest resources in storage capacity in order to reduce uncertainty. A degree of risk of inefficient resource usage is accepted as a tradeoff.

Risk-management behavior can be seen at many levels of living systems. All living systems maintain some stocks of materials for construction and energy production. Human individuals, groups, organizations, and societies are particularly active in increasing their storage and memory capacity. In fact, the ability of human systems to expand their storage capacity seems almost unlimited. This observation raises the question of whether there are any natural or logical limits to a system's storage capacity.

Two fields in which this question has been studied extensively are finance and operations management. At the level of organizations, particularly business firms, there has been much study of such questions as how much cash should be retained and how much credit is needed to support a given level of activity. Similarly, various models have been developed to calculate the optimal level of inventory of raw materials and finished goods. Nevertheless, controversy and disagreement still exist concerning these matters. The literature on just-in-time (JIT) production illustrates the issues involved in trying to determine an optimal trade-off between uncertainty and inefficiency.

JIT is a technique developed by Japanese manufacturers to improve the firm's efficiency by reducing its investment in inventory. Through extensive planning of resource needs and close monitoring of suppliers and production schedules, the firm is able to receive raw materials and components only days or hours before they are actually required, and to move materials smoothly through a multistage production process with minimal delay between stages. Even finished product inventory may be minimized by careful coordination of production with market demand. The technique also involves flexible use of machinery and employees. Overtime capacity and capability of rapid switchover from one product to another are used as buffers.[7]

Advocates of JIT point out its advantage of greater efficiency. Critics contend that this efficiency is attained at the expense of other systems. Suppliers may have to carry additional inventory themselves in order to meet the demands of their contract. Managers must devote additional time to planning and data gathering, and operative employees must be willing to work overtime. Machinery and transport may require upgrading. Also, the firm may face added risk from natural catastrophe or labor unrest.

Thus far there is no clear answer as to what constitutes the optimal trade-off between efficiency and risk reduction, from the point of view of the firm or the broader economic system of which it is a part. In stable times, however, JIT techniques seem to offer a competitive advantage.

At the societal level, there is debate about optimal storage capacity of natural resources and arms. Ecologists argue for increased stockpiling of nonrenewable resources through substitution of renewable resources, but economists point out the short-run market inefficiencies of such substitutions. Advocates of increased spending on national defense emphasize that investment in arms and armies reduces the risk of attack, whereas opponents contend that such spending on nonproductive goods and services undermines the strength of the economy.[8]

At all of these levels of living systems the basic trade-off appears to be the same: a degree of efficiency is sacrificed for the sake of reducing the uncertainty faced by the system. Uncertainty cannot be reduced to zero, however, and the cost of its reduction increases rapidly. It appears that unlimited growth of storage capacity is not good for the system, but a formula for the optimal trade-off has not yet been determined. Meanwhile, human systems continue to develop new means of storage and to expand existing capacity. Yet resistance has developed toward further spending on storage capacity, and there is increasing concern for efficiency in organizations.

Managers should be aware of the trade-offs between storage capacity and efficiency, and should be careful about going to extremes in either direction.

One of the forces that may cause managers to develop storage capacity beyond the immediate needs of the organization is that excess resources are a source of power. Let us now examine how this is so.

POWER

Power is a topic dear to the hearts of managers. It represents the capacity to control other people and systems, to cause them to do our bidding. But that is not what power is; that is what it potentially does.

Power lies in possession or control of excess resources and the dependency of other systems on those resources. Even if we were talking about batteries, this statement of the power concept would be correct. The power of a battery lies in its possession of excess electrons that are needed to activate an electrical device. To distinguish electrical power from power over people and social systems, let us call the latter social power.

Social Power

Social power may be defined in general as "possession or control of resources that the holder regards as excess, where the holder is a person or social system."[9] Note that resources do not convey power to us if we need them, ourselves, or if the resources are already earmarked for other purposes.

One of the reasons that efficiency is prized so highly is that efficient operations free up resources. These resources are then available as bases of power. Note, also, that excess or availability is a matter of perception. If we believe that certain dollars are already committed to buy new machinery, then they are not available for salary increases. If a firm cannot bear the thought of sharing certain trade secrets, then a joint venture may not be possible.

Although excess resources give us power in general, they might not do so in a particular relationship. If the question is whether system A has power over system B, that depends on whether B has needs for any of the resources that A controls. Indeed, what A possesses might not even be resources to B. If B is a horse, then person A's control of spendable money doesn't directly give A any power over B. Only by using the money to buy sugar cubes or a whip does A gain power over B in this case. Note, by the way, that A's resources may have positive or negative worth for B. That is, the horse can be rewarded with sugar or punished by lashes from the whip. Only a neutrally valued resource—in this case, money—carries no power.

Finally, in order for power to be effective, it must be perceived by both systems. System A must believe it has excess resources that B wants (or wants to avoid), and B must perceive that A controls those resources, that they have positive or negative worth, and that A is willing to use them or part with them.

French and Raven defined the following five common bases of social power:

1. *reward* power, based on B's perception that A has the ability to mediate rewards for B;
2. *coercive* power, based on B's perception that A has the ability to mediate punishments for B;
3. *legitimate* power, based on B's perception that A has a right to prescribe behavior for B;
4. *referent* power, based on B's identification (i.e., perception of oneness) with A; and
5. *expert* power, based on B's perception that A has special knowledge or expertise.[10]

Note that each of these power bases must be perceived by B in order for them to have any effect. French and Raven's five bases of social power have been well accepted by other writers, but the requirement of perception has often been ignored.

Another basis of social power is *obligation*, based on B's perception that A has already rewarded B and that B owes A a similar reward. Blau cited the development of obligations as a primary source of a manager's power.[11]

Finally, the willingness to exercise power, although not a resource or base of power in itself, is a necessary condition for its effectiveness. Many a battle has been lost to inferior forces because the commander was unwilling to commit his troops to the fray. The conditions that determine the effectiveness of social power are summed up in Figure 4-4.

Managers who wish to wield power are usually aware of the resources they hold, although they may not correctly perceive the value of those resources to others. For instance, a supervisor may know that she has the authority to discharge an employee for pilferage, but may incorrectly assume that the employee cares whether he is discharged or not. A salesman may know that he has a good product, but may be unaware of how much the customer wants it.

Perceptions about the availability of a resource may also pose problems. A manager may know that there is sufficient money in the budget to afford giving a raise to a superior employee, but may be very reluctant

Figure 4-4
Social Power Flow Chart

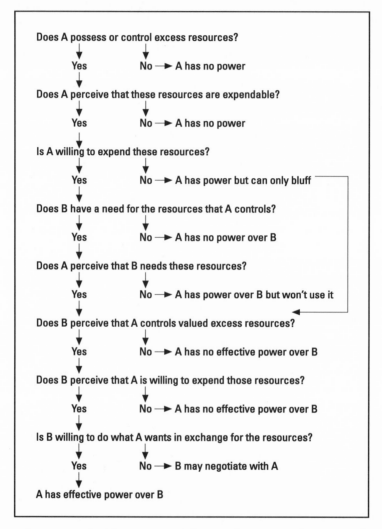

to use the money for that purpose. An employee may be aware that her supervisor has the authority to recommend her for a promotion, but may perceive that the supervisor is unwilling to exercise that authority on her behalf. Whether these perceptions are correct or not, they effectively cut off power.

A wise manager recognizes the limits of power. What you can reasonably ask employees to do depends on how much you are paying them, whether they like their work and their association with the firm, how long they have been a member, how much help you can give them, and how they regard you. Other exchange relationships such as family demands and legal constraints also limit power.

Two-Way Power

Thus far, I have discussed power as a one-way phenomenon, that is, the power of A over B. In the typical dyad, however, both systems have power, as indicated by the reciprocal flow of resources. We might then ask whether one side has *more* power than the other.

We could talk about A's *net power* as the result of subtracting B's power over A from A's power over B. But this would in many instances be misleading. Net power may vary from moment to moment, depending on what each system wants from the other. When A wants B to carry out an important task, A may be more willing to commit resources. On the other hand, B's power is increased by A's need for B's cooperation. Effective net power fluctuates according to the desires and perceptions of both systems.

A manager must assess power with respect to what is wanted from a particular person or social system at a particular time.

Systems A and B in the preceding discussion might be at any level; for example, two business firms, two managers, a firm and its employees, or a firm and the government. Social power is important to the firm, to individual managers, and to employees as a group. Each of these levels seeks power for its own purposes. The firm wants power over government regulators, competitors, suppliers, customers, and employees. Managers desire power over the firm, colleagues, and subordinates. Employees may organize a labor union in order to gain power over supervisors and the firm. Thus, social power is a multifaceted topic insofar as organizations are concerned.

The use of power to get things done involves communication, both to indicate what action is desired and to overcome inaccuracies of perception. Terms of exchange are often decided by a process of negotiation. The use of communication for influence and for agreement on terms of exchange is discussed at length in Chapter 5.

PRACTICAL CONSIDERATIONS

In a typical medium- or large-sized organization, resource management is divided among several departments. For materials there may be a purchasing department for acquisition, receiving and shipping departments for the input and output functions, materials handling and warehousing departments for distribution and storage, production departments for various stages of manufacture, a sales department for exchange, and a sanitation department to take care of wastes.

All of these departments deal with information, as well, but there are people and departments that specialize in information handling. Managers, secretaries, clerks, receptionists, lawyers, researchers, librarians, and computer programmers generally deal more with information than with matter-energy. Departments such as marketing, accounting, finance, public relations, and legal services specialize in processing information.

Money is the specialty of the accounting, finance, payroll, and budgeting departments. People are the province of the human resources department, the health and safety department, and line managers.

With so many departments involved in various aspects of resource management, suboptimization and lack of coordination become major concerns. Thus:

Top management must think clearly about resource needs and priorities, and must communicate these matters to those whose decisions will be affected. Trade-offs between efficiency and storage must be examined. In large organizations, it may be desirable to establish a position specifically to coordinate all aspects of resource management.

SUMMARY

Living systems regularly require resource inputs in order to survive. Business firms, for example, demand inputs of matter (e.g., machinery, raw materials), energy, information (about competitors, customer needs, new technology, the economy), people (e.g., employees, customers), and money.

Because many resources are scarce and costly, efficient use of inputs is also essential for survival and success. Efficiency of the system can be increased by reducing the cost of resource consumption and/or by increasing the worth of the system and its outputs. Although managers often focus on cost cutting, the performance of the system is equally important.

Efficient operations free up resources as a source of power. Systems also store resources toward future needs, even though this creates some inefficiency. Storage in the form of buffer stocks increases power and reduces the risk of long-term deprivation of vital resources.

Power lies in possession or control of excess resources. The effectiveness of our power for purposes of influence over other systems depends on (1) availability of resources, (2) our perception of their availability, (3) our willingness to use them, (4) the effectiveness of our communication concerning our power and what we want from the other system, (5) the other system's perception of its needs and our power to fulfill them, and (6) the countervailing power held by the other system.

In order to increase their power, managers must

1. *acquire or obtain control of resources that they do not need and that have value to others;*
2. *communicate their control of these resources and their willingness to use them;*
3. *be ready to use their power to back up their communications;* and
4. *reduce their own dependency on resources owned or controlled by others, or at least communicate that they are not dependent.*

Most of the resources required by higher-level living systems are acquired from other living systems. Consequently, social systems are engaged in a very complex web of resource exchange. Both parties in an exchange usually hold power. Thus, the terms of most exchange relationships are negotiated and mutually agreed upon. Money is used in lieu of other resources in order to facilitate such exchanges.

NOTES

1. Lane Tracy, *The Living Organization: Systems of Behavior* (New York: Praeger, 1989), 48.

2. Jay W. Forrester, *Industrial Dynamics* (Cambridge, MA: MIT Press, 1961).

3. James G. Miller, *Living Systems* (New York: McGraw-Hill, 1978), 41.

4. Ibid., 101.

5. Thierry C. Pauchant and Ian I. Mitroff, *Transforming the Crisis-Prone Organization: Preventing Individual, Organizational and Environmental Tragedies* (San Francisco: Jossey-Bass, 1992).

6. James D. Thompson, *Organizations in Action* (New York: McGraw-Hill, 1967).

7. Yasuhiro Monden, "Adaptable Kanban system helps Toyota maintain just-in-time production," *Industrial Engineering* 13, no. 5 (1981): 29–46.

8. Paul Kennedy, *The Rise and Fall of the Great Powers* (New York: Random House, 1987).

9. Tracy, *Living Organization*, 124.

10. John R. P. French and Bertram Raven, "The bases of social power," in D. Cartwright (Ed.), *Studies in Social Power* (Ann Arbor: University of Michigan, 1959), 150–67.

11. Peter M. Blau, *Exchange and Power in Social Life* (New York: Wiley, 1964).

Chapter 5

Managing Information Flow

A Montero Virtual Realty (MVR) customer, Sarah Sealy, complained that she wasn't shown a house that would have interested her very much. She only learned about it from a friend after it was sold to someone else.

After checking with the sales staff, Alex learned that half of them hadn't known about the house, because it had only been listed two days before it was sold. The salesperson who had been showing houses to Mrs. Sealy was also surprised that she would be interested in that house; it didn't fit the profile they had worked up for her. But the profile might not be accurate; Mrs. Sealy had never seen or approved it. Alex wants to know how this sort of mixup can be avoided in the future.

Failure to receive important information and lack of feedback are common problems in managing information flow. Other potential problems include inadequate or excessive amounts of information in the system, outdated or inaccurate information, biases in processing information, and blocked or clogged channels. These are very serious problems, given that the "business" of organizations is increasingly the processing of information.[1]

In Chapter 2 we dealt very briefly with the required information processes that must be built into a new organization. This chapter examines these processes in more detail, looks at the structures associated with them, and considers the problems that may develop with them. We first examine how information is processed in living organizations. We then use that understanding as a platform to examine such topics as assignment of information-processing responsibilities, control of processes, and organizational learning. Finally, we develop a communications model based on living systems concepts and use the model to examine pathologies of the process.

INFORMATION PROCESSING

Can you imagine a life form that does not use or process information? How would it control and coordinate its own processes in order to attain its purposes and goals? How could it monitor and respond to its environment? It is easy to see why the ability to process information is essential to living systems.

The genetic templates of cells, organs, and organisms automatically provide for development of subsystems that process information. The innate communication capabilities of organisms form a basis for information processing within groups and organizations, as well. Yet a social system cannot simply depend on the information processing abilities of its individual members. There must be information-processing subsystems that operate for the social system, not just for its organic components. The design and maintenance of such subsystems for an organization is the responsibility of its founders and managers.

Process and Structure

Miller defines a living system's *structure* as "the arrangement of its subsystems and components in three-dimensional space at a given moment of time."[2] Structure may change from moment to moment, but social systems usually have certain structures that remain relatively stable for long periods of time. Managers tend to focus on the design of these relatively stable structures although, as we will see, it may also be necessary to manage the change of structure.

Regardless of the speed of change, we may take a snapshot that captures the structure of the system at a given instant. Yet this ability to freeze the action, so to speak, should not mislead us into thinking that structure is necessarily stable. It is stable only to the extent that the system is able to maintain it as a steady state.

Process is dynamic. It is defined as "all change over time of matter-energy or information in a system."[3] If structure is represented in a snapshot, process is like a movie or video. A video records *history,* a set of changes that have already occurred within the system and cannot readily be reversed.[4]

Critical subsystems are defined by the processes that they carry out. Let us now reexamine the processes carried out by each of the critical information-processing subsystems of an organization. We also look at organizational structures that are often associated with these processes.

Critical Information-Processing Subsystems in Organizations

Reproducer. An organization's reproducer subsystem is involved in transmission of information, which becomes the template of a new system similar to the organization. Except in a few organizations, such as franchising firms, reproduction is a sporadic activity. Thus, it may be assigned to a temporary structure such as a task force. Because we have already discussed this subsystem extensively in Chapter 2, it is not treated further here.

Boundary. The boundary subsystem carries out three essential processes. The first is to contain and bind together the components that make up the system. Second, the boundary protects these components from environmental stresses. Third, it acts as a gatekeeper, excluding or permitting entry to various sorts of matter-energy and information.[5] The third process definitely involves information processing, and the other two processes may do so.

In an organization, the boundary consists of people and artifacts. Certain members or employees are assigned roles that involve direct interface with the environment. At NewVent, trainers give new recruits a common vocabulary and a set of rules for working within the system, in order to bind employees together. Guards and receptionists greet people who are seeking to enter the premises of the organization, either admitting them or denying admission and thereby protecting the system from unwanted visitors. Mailroom personnel sort incoming mail and packages, rejecting material that is misaddressed or unwanted. Secretaries screen telephone calls, rejecting callers who would only waste the time of executives but giving priority to important calls. Credit checkers approve or reject applicants for credit based on information about their credit rating.

Members of the organization perform most of the acts involved in protecting the organization from environmental stresses and excluding or receiving information. Note, however, that these people are spread throughout the organization. Most of the members who engage in boundary processes are involved with other critical subsystems as well. There is typically no single department associated with the boundary subsystem, although protection may be the primary duty of a security department. Boundary functions may also be dispersed to other organizations such as a secretarial service or a security agency.

Artifacts are involved in all of the boundary functions. The process of containing the organization is performed primarily by artifacts. Gates, fences, walls, roofs, floors, doors, windows, and vehicles are used to contain both the members and the equipment of the organization. Counters and docks, alarms and gauges, telephones, computers, and software are employed as aids in screening inputs and protecting the system from intrusions.

Input transducer. The input transducer is the subsystem of sensors that bring markers bearing information into the system, changing them into other forms suitable for transmission within the system.[6] Members of an organization are the primary components of its input transducer. Their eyes, ears, noses, taste buds, and touch sensors receive large volumes of information. After sorting and evaluating this information, some of it is put into words orally, in writing, or in computer code for transmission within the system.

Artifacts also play an important role. Telephones receive electrical impulses and transform them into sound waves. TV cameras receive light waves, transforming them into electrical impulses for transmission to monitors. Computers receive magnetic impulses and change them into electrical impulses for processing and transmission within a network.

Groups and departments that are in close contact with the environment of an organization are part of the input transducer. Sales representatives at NewVent receive oral orders and put them in writing on the proper forms or enter them into a computer terminal. The marketing department collects information on responses to new products and advertising campaigns. Research and development (R&D) personnel scan scientific journals for new technological developments.

Some firms disperse part of the process to other organizations. Airlines put their computer terminals directly in the offices of travel agents. MVR depends on the Virtual Realty network to gather information about available properties in distant cities.

Internal transducer. The internal transducer subsystem is similar to the input transducer, except that it receives information-bearing markers from subsystems or components within the system. The focus of the internal transducer is on information about significant changes in subsystems or components. As with the input transducer, the markers may be changed to other matter-energy forms that can be transmitted within the system.[7]

Supervisors generally serve as the primary human components of the internal transducer in organizations. They receive information through their eyes and ears about changes in work behavior, machine processes, information flow, product quality, production orders, benefits, budgets, policies, and procedures. They may then put this information in other forms to be transmitted upward or downward in the hierarchy. Other groups that specialize in internal transducing include the human resources department, internal auditors, budget analysts, operations analysts, and quality-control inspectors.

Parts of the process may be dispersed to labor union stewards, consultants, and external auditors. Artifacts of the internal transducer subsystem may include TV cameras, heat sensors and smoke alarms, punch clocks, feedback sensors on automated production lines, thermostats, and computerized inventory control systems.

Channel and net. The channel and net subsystem carries information-bearing markers around the system. Channels intersect at points called nodes or deciders. "If at a junction information is passed on unchanged, that junction is a node; if it is reduced in amount or altered by such adjustment processes as omission, error, filtering, abstracting, or choice among alternatives, the junction is a decider."[8] For example, a clerk who simply receives paperwork, records it, and passes it on to the next station is acting as a node. But a clerk who chooses whether or to whom to pass on the paperwork is a decider. Nets are formed by multiple channels and junctions.

Key human components of the channel and net subsystem at NewVent and other organizations include clerks, secretaries, messengers, and supervisors, each of whom may act as nodes or deciders in the net.

Managers may assume that clerks and secretaries act as nodes when, in fact, these people frequently filter and alter information before passing it on. A wise manager knows that, at times, anyone and everyone in the network acts as a decider.

Many organizations now have local area networks of computers and terminals. Other artifacts include telephone and intercom lines, pneumatic tubes, and mail boxes. Large, multisite organizations like UniGlobe and the Virtual Realty network disperse parts of their channel and net to telecommunications firms and mail systems.

Timer. System processes must be temporally coordinated with each other and with events in the environment. The timer subsystem generates and transmits timing signals to the decider of the system and to subsystem deciders. These timing signals may be coordinated with states of the environment (e.g., day or night, summer or winter) or of system components (e.g., process completion, queue length).[9]

The timer process in organizations is carried out primarily by artifacts. Clocks and bells or buzzers signal the start and end of work periods. Calendars determine the cycle of reports, distribution of wages and dividends, and, in some cases, product changes. At MVR, for instance, the calendar determines when a private listing becomes a multiple listing. Moving belts on a production line set the pace of work. Electric timers or computers control the length of time that bread is baked in a mechanized bakery.

People are also involved in the timer process. Supervisors and managers set deadlines and urge employees to work faster or permit them to slow down, according to the needs of the organization. Employees may also be trained to pace themselves. For example, McDonald's chefs are instructed to cook each hamburger for a preset length of time. Timing devices also require people to maintain and reset them periodically.

Ultimately, the signals that control organizational timers come from outside the system. Electric timing devices are controlled by current cycles generated by an electric utility. Daily and annual rhythms are tied to natural cycles of the sun and moon. Parts of the calendar, such as holidays, are determined by the government. Government radio signals may be used to reset clocks.

Decoder. Every organization has its own internal codes for information transmission within the system. For example, NewVent uses the English language as its primary code, to which it adds certain proprietary terms. The decoder alters the code of information from the input transducer or internal transducer into this "private" code.[10]

The Virtual Realty network uses a digital code to transmit the pictures and other data that are decoded by their interactive video equipment. Other examples of information input requiring decoding would include letters and telephone calls in foreign languages, oral reports from non-English-speaking employees, and technical information from competitors and government agencies.

The decoding process in organizations is carried out by individuals and, increasingly, by computers. Large international organizations may have a special group of foreign-language translators, but may disperse part of the task to embassy personnel. A considerable amount of decoding of technical terms and jargon is dispersed to individuals throughout the organization.

Associator. The associator subsystem forms enduring associations among items of information in the system. This is the first stage of the learning process.[11] By associating information about billing and payment dates, for example, NewVent may learn that certain customers always pay their bills late.

The association process is dispersed downward to individual members and groups within the system. Salespeople at MVR attempt to link data about available properties with profiles of customer desires. Accountants and statisticians form associations among bits of financial and operational data; supervisors may associate production data with schedules and budgets.

The process is aided by computer programs, forms, and filing systems. Work stations may be laid out in a way that aids operators in associating parts with their places in an assembly. Some associating of data may be dispersed outward to consultants.

Memory. The memory subsystem stores various sorts of information for different periods of time. The process involves three stages: (a) storing information-bearing markers, (b) maintaining them, and (c) retrieving the information. Memory is the second stage of the learning process.[12]

Every member of an organization stores information for the organization, but members higher in the hierarchy tend to store more of it. In addition, certain groups of people such as bookkeepers, secretaries, clerks, librarians, and computer operators may be charged with special duties in the storage, maintenance, and retrieval of information.

Libraries, books, files, filing cabinets, appointment calendars, video and audio tapes, films, disks, and computers are artifacts employed by the organizational memory. Some memory processes may be dispersed to other organizations such as banks, public libraries, government data banks, and public accounting firms. Some of NewVent's financial records are retained by UniGlobe.

Decider. The decider is "the executive subsystem which receives information inputs from all other subsystems and transmits to them information outputs that control the entire system."[13] This subsystem was discussed at length in Chapters 2 and 3 and is examined again in Chapter 9. Here we only note some of its specific processes and structures.

Computers may aid the deciding process in an organization, but the primary components of an organization's decider subsystem are its members and member groups such as task forces and committees. In large corporations like UniGlobe, the decider subsystem consists of many echelons, with the Board of Directors at the top. Yet every member of the organization must make decisions for it.

Deciding is the only process that cannot be fully dispersed outward from the system. This means that when individuals or committees make a decision for an organization, they must do so on the basis of their understanding of the organization's purposes and goals, not on some other basis. If an organization cannot make its own decisions in this way, it ceases to be an independent entity, although it may continue to exist as a component of another living system.

Although an organization cannot fully disperse the deciding process, it may do so temporarily or partially. For example, a court-appointed executor may make decisions for the organization during bankruptcy proceedings. A management firm may make and implement decisions under general guidelines from the owners of a business. Decisions about new technology at MVR are made by the headquarters of the network, and UniGlobe makes some budgeting decisions for NewVent.

Encoder. The encoder subsystem reverses the process of the decoder, altering the code of information from the system's "private" code to one that can be interpreted by other systems.[14] In an organization, the encoding process would likely be assigned to many of the same members, groups, and artifacts that are involved in decoding. MVR's video equipment may be seen as decoding digital signals for the organization or as encoding them into pictures for the clients. From the organization's point of view, however, advertising and public relations specialists would be much more involved in encoding than in decoding, whereas economists and market researchers would tend to focus on the decoding process.

Output transducer. The output transducer subsystem transmits markers bearing information from the system. In the process it changes the system's markers into other forms of matter-energy.[15] In an organization, for instance, handwritten notes and dictation are changed into typewritten letters or computer files that can be transmitted by mail or electronically. Sales representatives change written materials into oral presentations.

Output transducing and encoding are often done together. For instance, the legal and accounting departments at UniGlobe not only translate organizational information into a more public language, but also transmit it in a format acceptable to government agencies.

Secretaries, mail clerks, salespeople, spokespersons, and computer users are likely to be involved in output transducing. The process may also be dispersed outwardly to bulk mailers, messenger services, advertising and public relations firms, and television personalities. Artifacts involved in this process include computers and software, modems, stationery, postage meters, radio transmitters, and store displays.

Table 5-1 summarizes the information-processing critical subsystems, organizational structures associated with them, and artifacts on which they frequently rely.

ASSIGNING RESPONSIBILITIES FOR INFORMATION FLOW

NewVent must be responsive to its environment, including its parent corporation. Thus, it must have people or departments whose responsibility is to gather information on such matters as availability of capital, budgets, and cash flow; availability and cost of various forms of energy, materials, human resources, and equipment; consumer preferences, price competition, market share, and new products; new materials and technologies; employee morale and suggestions; public opinion; corporate expectations and policies; and government rules and regulations. It must also have people and departments responsible for manipulating and transforming these information inputs into forms that are more valuable to NewVent or its customers. And there must be people or departments whose task is to disseminate information to customers, clients, agents, suppliers, the parent company, government agencies, the media, and the public.

Table 5-1
Information-Processing Subsystems, Structures, Artifacts

Subsystem	Department or Group	Dispersed to:	Artifacts
Reproducer	Board of Directors overseas operations	legal firm construction firm	buildings equipment
Boundary	Security Department secretaries	police credit bureau	fence, gate alarms
Input transducer	Sales, Marketing, R&D	each member marketing firm	telephones computers
Internal transducer	Personnel Department supervisors	union stewards consultants	TV cameras computers
Channel and net	supervisors secretaries	telephone firms mail systems	phone lines computers
Timer	supervisors managers	electric utility nature	clocks calender
Decoder	translators technical specialists	embassy employees each member	dictionary code books
Associator	Accounting Department statisticians	consultants each member	computers file system
Memory	bookkeepers librarians	public libraries banks	books, file tapes, disks
Decider	Board of Directors executives, managers	each member	computers
Encoder	Public Relations Dept. translators	advertising firm	dictionary
Output transducer	Sales Department mail room	marketing firms bulk mailing firms	displays stationery

Source: Lane Tracy, "Design for organizational health," *Journal of Business Research* no. 12 (1992), 19. Used by permission of the Research Institute Administration Office, College of Economics, Nihon University, Tokyo, Japan.

The Duty of Gathering

Sources of information vary widely. Consequently, in all but the smallest organizations the task of gathering information must be divided up and allocated to various components. In NewVent, this means assigning to the marketing manager the task of collecting data about consumer preferences, price competition, and the like. The production manager is given responsibility for monitoring employee morale, keeping track of inventory, and knowing how much productive capacity is available. There is a purchasing specialist in charge of collecting data about the cost and availability of raw materials, capital goods, and supplies. Information about cost and availability of human resources is gathered by members of the personnel staff. A small accounting group has the responsibility of monitoring cash flow and comparing expenditures against the budget, as well as collecting and compiling data on costs and profits. Finally, the chief executive officer (CEO) retains the tasks of monitoring public opinion, keeping track of new products and processes, and watching out for changes in government regulations.

In a larger organization the responsibility for various categories of information would probably be allocated to functional departments. Table 5-2 shows such a distribution of information-gathering responsibility.

The term "gathering" implies an active search for information. Some information, however, is simply received. Examples of such information would be invoices and bills, inquiries from potential customers or suppliers, employment applications, and news from the media. In any case, a component of the organization that gathers or receives data is acting as part of the *input transducer subsystem*, carrying the information across the boundary into the system.

Some components also act as part of the *internal transducer*, gathering or receiving information from other components of the system. Members of the auditing department, for instance, are assigned the task of gathering financial data from other departments in order to monitor the use of funds. Human resource management specialists may be expected to conduct job satisfaction surveys and exit interviews in order to assess employee morale.

The basic point of this discussion is that

The designer/manager of an organization must identify all of the kinds of information that are required for proper functioning of the system, and must assign the collection of each kind of information to some component of the organization.

Having all of the components gathering all kinds of information would be too inefficient and chaotic. On the other hand, failing to gather certain kinds of information might be fatal to the organization. For example, if MVR fails to bring in new listings, it will soon go out of business.

Table 5-2
Organizational Distribution of Information-Gathering Duties

Department	Information-gathering duties
Accounting	Costs, financial transactions, expenditures, receipts, depreciation.
Engineering	New machines--costs and capabilities, new technology, machine performance data, maintenance data.
Finance	Debts, availability of credit, interest rates and trends, stock prices and trends, cash flow.
Human resources	Employee dossiers, rates of absenteeism and turnover, records of accidents and illness, employee discipline, labor availability, grievances, arbitrator's decisions, training, insurance and pension data, regular work hours and overtime hours, rates of pay.
Information systems	New hardware and software, information needs, system capacity and utilization, costs, viruses and system security.
Legal	Patent infringement, trademark protection, adherence to regulations, law suits and vulnerability, liability, new laws and regulations.
Marketing	Consumer preferences, market share, advertising rates and coverage, demographics, reactions to test marketing and gimmicks, availability of production capacity.
Production	Utilization of machine time and employee hours, scrap rates, machine maintenance, process controls.
Public relations	Polls, media coverage, editorials, complaints, legislative activities, industry trends.
Research and development	New materials, new production processes, new applications, scientific advances and breakthroughs, improvements in existing materials and processes.
Sales	Customer response to new products, customer needs, new orders, frequency of calls, complaints, expenses.

As parts of a transducer subsystem, each of the components assigned to an information-gathering function should represent easy points of entry, points at which little energy is required to bring the data across the boundary of the organization or from one department to another. In practice, this means that these components must be in regular contact with the sources of information and must be very familiar with the types of information produced by those sources. It would make no sense, for instance, to assign an accountant to gather data about market penetration or an engineer to do a personnel audit.

The principle of efficiency demands, in general, that overlaps in responsibility for information gathering be minimized. Nevertheless, certain types of information may be of such critical importance that a degree of redundancy is justified. For example, shifts in consumer preferences are so important in industries such as fashion, toys, and cosmetics that firms in these industries should expect their designers, marketers, and sales representatives all to keep their eyes and ears open for trends in the market. A new subsidiary like NewVent is so dependent on the parent corporation that everyone who has contact with headquarters should be instructed to be alert for cues from their counterparts. All employees at MVR should be on the watch for properties that may come on the market.

Gathering information is only the first step. Other issues that must be considered include: To what extent will the gatherers filter the information before passing it on? Who will decode the information? Where will it be sent within the system, and when? What media will be used? Which components are responsible for the processes of association, memory, and deciding?

Filtering

Rarely is information fed into the channel and net in full, just as it is received. If all collectors of information did this, the system would quickly become overloaded. Thus, information gatherers and transducers must also be delegated the *boundary* duty of filtering information, choosing what to allow into the system and what to discard.

> *Because filtering, if done improperly, can lead to the loss of important data, it is advisable to provide detailed instructions as to what information should be retained. At the very least the gatherers must have a clear understanding of the goals of the system so that they can make good judgments about what information to accept and what to reject.*

When the same filtering decisions must be made repeatedly, it is more efficient to program them by providing specific criteria for acceptance and rejection. The instructions should also include procedures for handling unusual information that does not fit the standard criteria. For instance, receptionists should be instructed to forward certain kinds of phone calls immediately, to put others on hold or ask them to call back, and politely refuse other calls. Unusual calls might be forwarded to an executive secretary for decisions on how to handle them.

Responsibility for Decoding

Many components of the organization may have the capability of decoding most of the information that is received. The managerial members of a business firm, for instance, will generally be able to decode accounting data, marketing statistics, budgets, employment statistics, and even government regulations, to some extent. But it is often most efficient to assign the gatherers of such information the additional task of decoding it into a form that is more readily usable by other components. Thus, for instance, economists who gather numerical data on economic projections may translate them into charts and graphs that are more easily understood by executives.

Sales representatives may enter data about sales orders onto a standard form or into a computer terminal, using alphanumeric codes keyed to inventory. Alternatively, the coding may be done by computer. For instance, fast food shops use order input terminals that translate icon keys into information that flows to a video terminal in the kitchen and also becomes a printed receipt for the customer.

Selecting Media and Recipients

Organizations typically have more than one medium or channel of internal transmission. Messages may be passed orally in person or by telephone, intercom, or "grapevine"; or they may be transmitted in written form on paper or by E-mail. The message may be directed to a single individual or broadcast to a group or a mailing list.

The sender must decide (1) which channel(s) to use, (2) whether multiple media are desirable, and (3) who needs to receive the information. In some cases, the sender may also have to decide who should *not* receive it. There may also be proper channels to go through. Some decisions about distribution may be the responsibility of a higher echelon in the system.

In choosing a medium, the sender must weigh the importance of speed and accuracy of transmission, as well as the volume of data to be transmitted, the desirability of feedback, and the cost of transmission. Information about a rapidly changing situation must be received immediately, if it is to have any value. When a machine breaks down, for example, you would not send a memo about it. You would probably talk to someone in person or by phone. Yet for transmitting the specifics of the problem, such as the exact parts involved, a written medium would offer less chance of error. Thus, you might choose to back up your oral communication with an E-mail message.

Large amounts of numerical data are best put in writing or presented graphically. A memo or report will suffice unless speed is also required. In the latter case, a direct transfer of data from one computer to another

might be the medium of choice. But you would not use such channels if
your primary interest is persuasion. In that case, you would want to use
multiple channels that transmit "rich" information and allow immediate
feedback. Person-to-person or group meetings would be a likely choice,
because they provide both aural and visual channels as well as opportunities for direct exchange of information.[16]

The cost of transmission is a complex matter. It includes not only the
energy cost of transmitting a message from one point to another, but also
the time cost to all of the people involved, and possibly the cost of occu-
pying a scarce channel at the expense of other messages. Taking up a key
executive's time with an oral message about a trivial matter may be quite
expensive in terms of opportunity costs. Tying up a phone line and
thereby blocking access by important customers could also be quite
costly. Solving problems such as this is a task often dispersed to a communications network consultant.

With respect to management of information processing the discussion
leads to the following recommendations:

1. *The organization should provide a variety of channels, consistent with calculations of the cost of having insufficient channels or the wrong kinds.*
2. *Employees should be trained in how and when to use these channels, and in
   weighing the costs.*

CONTROL

Many processes are controlled by means of feedback. That is, information is gathered on outcomes of these processes and is compared with
goals or subgoals to ascertain whether the process is proceeding according to plan. If it isn't, corrections are made in the plan or the process. In
addition, a new plan may be needed to correct the erroneous outcomes.

Organizations often assign the control process to specific individuals
and groups such as auditors and quality control inspectors. Indeed, control of processes may be the primary task of these components. Nevertheless, many writers are now calling for a change in our thinking about
control. They are advocating a broader concept of control and involvement of more members in the process.

Control processes are a common phenomenon in business firms. Managers are generally well aware of the application of statistical controls to
the production process and to the testing of raw materials and subassemblies as well. Discipline, as administered by supervisors and the human
resources department, is an attempt to exercise control over deviant
behavior. Bureaucracies go well beyond these steps by applying standard
policies and procedures to control information flow, decision making,

storage, channels of communication, and many other organizational processes.

Yet today the bureaucratic model is under attack as being too rigid and unresponsive to an organization's overall purposes and goals. Although the need for control still exists, there is a shift away from micromanagement (except in the public sector, where accountability is king) and toward control of processes based on a broad understanding of organizational goals and purposes.[17]

Furthermore, control of the production process is undergoing a revolution based on variants of the Deming method and the use of computer-controlled machinery. Deming emphasizes a fourteen-point agenda aimed at continuous improvement of processes, not control aimed simply at returning outcomes to a fixed range.[18]

The new concept of control as "continuous improvement" is in keeping with our view that living systems are dynamic, not static. As we see in Chapter 10, organizations *must* change to keep up with a rapidly changing world. Controls that simply return the system to the status quo are no longer adequate, if they ever were.

Another shift in thinking is that continuous improvement is everyone's business. No longer is control narrowly assigned to specialists. All employees are encouraged to monitor processes and suggest ways in which they could be improved in furtherance of organizational goals of efficiency, effectiveness, better service, cost savings, and profits. The assumptions are that many eyes, minds, and viewpoints are better than a few, that those who are involved in particular processes know the most about them, and that all members understand and accept the goals of the organization.

ORGANIZATIONAL LEARNING

The concept of continuous improvement is being applied not only to products and services but also to the components of the system.[19] Most people are capable of doing much more than organizations typically ask them to. But some progressive firms are finding that cross-training employees and asking them to perform a variety of duties greatly improves the flexibility and responsiveness of the organization.[20] Money spent on training and education is considered an investment, not an expense.

The ability to learn is as important at the organizational level as it is for individual success. We see all around us the effects on business firms that have been slow to learn or to adapt to changing conditions. IBM encountered large financial losses and had to downsize rapidly because it did not react quickly enough to the trend toward smaller computers. Likewise, General Motors was slow to adapt to changing competition and lost substantial ground not only to Japanese automakers but also to its faster-learning rivals, Ford and Chrysler.

Organizations must learn from experience so that they can improve their performance. They must also respond to changes in their environment. According to Peters and Toffler, the need for organizations to be flexible and adaptive has become increasingly acute in today's rapidly changing world.[21]

Organizational learning involves the organization's input and internal transducers, channel and net, decoder, associator, decider, and memory. Data about the environment and outcomes are collected and fed to components of the decider subsystem who analyze the data and compare it with previous experience, formulate new responses or actions and implement them, and record the decision.[22] All of this should be done on a continuous or regularly recurring basis.

Managers must establish a system for organizational learning. Adaptation should be a regular part of the organization's processes.

Peters provides numerous examples of organizations that have done this.[23] In many cases, it involves removing layers of bureaucracy and involving lower echelons of the decider subsystem in the process. In other words, learning occurs throughout the organization, if you let it. The most important role for management may be to see that learning, wherever it occurs in the system, is transmitted throughout the firm.

Returning to the problem that was presented at the beginning of the chapter, Alex needs to make sure that MVR learns from the customer's complaint. At the most superficial level, Alex might simply order that all salespeople check for new listings at the beginning of every day. By involving the salespeople in seeking a solution, however, Alex might gain not only a better plan but also a greater willingness among employees to seek and solve other problems. The salespeople, using their perspective and understanding of the problem, might suggest that new listings be displayed for a day in a special place before they are incorporated into the regular book. They might then go on to suggest ways in which they could keep an eye out for possible new listings.

A deeper level of learning would be represented by Alex setting up a regular staff meeting at which problems are raised and solutions are sought. Training could be provided in problem-solving techniques. A bulletin board or newsletter might be used to disseminate the results.

Many firms have done something similar under the rubric of quality circles (QC), total quality management (TQM), or some other acronym. Although these programs are often considered to be fads, they contain a core of truth about organizational success today. Modern organizations must institutionalize some means of learning and adapting to change, and this usually means involving people at all levels of the system.

COMMUNICATION

We are accustomed to thinking of communication as an exchange of information *between* systems, and it is. But communication also occurs between components *within* systems. Communication is the backbone of information processing in organizations.

Figure 5-1
Model of Communication between Two Living Systems

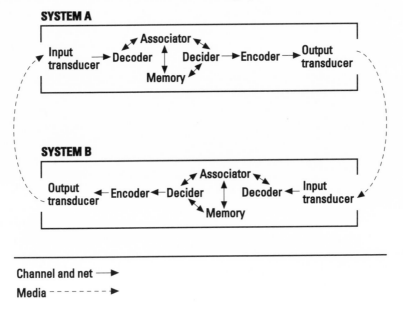

Figure 5-1 displays a simple model of communication between two living systems. Let us assume that the two systems are members of the same organization. Member A decides to send a message to B. The message is passed through neural channels, encoded in standard English, and transmitted orally. Member B perceives the message, decodes it into neural impulses, and employs memory and association to put it in context and make "sense" out of it. That might be sufficient but, in order to acknowledge receipt of the message and check on interpretation, B may transmit a message to A in return, as shown.

We can see in this model several points at which the process might break down. In encoding the message, A might not correctly anticipate how B will react to various words. Even among native speakers of a common language, vocabularies differ greatly, and words have different learned connotations for each person. Furthermore, member A might not speak distinctly or might not say precisely what he intends to say.

To overcome such problems A may repeat the message, confirm it in writing, or try to convey it over the "grapevine." Facial expressions and body language also play a part in supporting (or sometimes disconfirming) a message. That is why face-to-face communication is regarded as a richer medium than written or telephonic communication.[24]

When the message arrives, member B might be hearing other things at the same time (i.e., noise) that interfere with accurate perception of the message, or might be attending to other sensory stimuli (e.g., hunger). Member B might also reject the message as being relatively unimportant or something she doesn't want to hear.[25] The message may be decoded differently than it was encoded, or the associations with the words may be different than expected. For instance, B may interpret the message as a request when A intended it as a command. Feedback, the return loop from B to A, may clear up many of these problems of communication, but it is subject to the same potential sources of error.

Communication between independent living systems can never be perfect. That is, the message will not be received as intended 100 percent of the time. Even if that were possible, it might not be good for the organization, because it would risk turning the members into automatons. Nonetheless, a high degree of effectiveness in communication is considered desirable because it increases cohesiveness, integration, and coordination among organizational components.

Other things being equal, the organization is more *efficient* if messages do not have to be repeated or sent through multiple channels, because such repetition requires expenditure of resources. The organization is also likely to be more *effective* if all voices are heard in formulating objectives and everyone is in basic agreement with these objectives, so that messages are readily accepted. The system is more *responsive* if messages can be relayed quickly and accurately to appropriate decision centers. Perhaps the organization is more *intelligent* as well.

ORGANIZATIONAL INTELLIGENCE

Although there is no standard measure of organizational intelligence, I believe that organizations are becoming smarter. We don't know all of the factors that affect intelligence, but data processing speed and accuracy as well as good memory must be important. Electronic devices have greatly accelerated data processing and have increased memory capacity. Furthermore, the ability of organizations to access data, both from memory and from the environment, has improved.

A subtler factor is the ability to associate data in order to create new meaning. This is affected by the speed of information flow, because greater flow increases the likelihood that data will collide. But association is also influenced by the number of ideas that can be processed at one time. Coprocessing is one method of increasing intelligence.

The intelligence of a bureaucracy is essentially limited by the intelligence of the key decision makers. Even if internal communication is accelerated electronically, all major decisions and associations are made by a few individuals. But newer forms of organization, such as matrix structure and adhocracy, emphasize shared decision making.[26]

When decisions are shared, coprocessing is involved and the collective ability to process a variety of ideas is increased. This ability has been enhanced by the development of group processing methods such as brainstorming, nominal group technique, the Delphi technique, and social judgment analysis.[27] These methods allow groups to separate the processes of association and decision so that new ideas can be generated freely before any analysis and choice is made. Indeed, it is easier for groups to separate these processes than for an individual to do so.

Further advances in organizational intelligence are likely. Computer memory and processing speed are still increasing. Computer networks, E-mail, and Fax machines have added fast new channels of communication, with voice mail, videophones, and other developments on the immediate horizon. Brainstorming, nominal groups, the Delphi technique, and social judgment analysis can each be computerized, with resultant improvements in speed, simultaneity of idea generation, and enforcement of rules. Finally, large organizations seem to be more and more inclined toward shared decision making, which has the potential of adding the intelligence of the organization to that of the individual members.

PATHOLOGIES OF INFORMATION PROCESSING

In order to diagnose problem situations and prescribe solutions, a manager needs to know what can go wrong with the organization's information-processing subsystems. Following is a partial list of pathologies with their symptoms and some suggested treatments:

1. Channels may be inadequate for the volume of information that is entering them. They may be too few, too narrow, or too slow. Symptoms: messages not getting through, arriving late or garbled. Possi-

ble treatments: Expand the number, size, or speed of channels (e.g., add phone lines); filter inputs more carefully.

2. Excessive or improper filtering of useful data. Symptoms: components not receiving the data they need. Possible treatments: Reduce the filtering and allow more raw data to reach the affected components; improve the decision rules used for filtering.

3. Inadequate filtering of useless or erroneous data. Symptoms: components being swamped by data they cannot use. Possible treatments: Increase the filtering by adding more levels of filtration; improve the decision rules used for filtering.

4. Excessive use of one-way channels of communication. Symptoms: instructions not carried out properly; receivers confused by messages; low morale. Possible treatments: Train senders to recognize when two-way channels are needed; provide more two-way channels; encourage receivers to open up channels on their own when confused.

5. Groupthink—members of decision-making groups losing their ability to evaluate ideas critically because of perceived group pressure for conformity.[28] Symptoms: illusions of group invulnerability; belief in inherent group morality; stereotyping competitors as weak, evil, and stupid; rationalization of unpleasant or disconfirming data; applying pressure to deviants to conform; self-censorship by members; illusions of unanimity; protecting group from hearing outside viewpoints. Possible treatments: Encourage group members to share objections; train group leaders to be impartial; assign competing groups to the same problem; require groups to solicit outside reactions; assign a group member as "devil's advocate."

Overall, although redundancy and excessive information processing can be serious problems, most organizations probably err on the side of too little information. The most successful organizations in many fields appear to be those that encourage open communication and broad dispersal of decision making responsibility throughout the membership. Furthermore, although information systems may initially dump too much data on managers, most organizations have learned to control this problem and have found ways to take advantage of the additional information that such systems can provide.

SUMMARY

Information flow in organizations and other living systems involves more than half of their critical subsystems. Organizational information flows through formal and informal networks of oral (i.e., face to face) and written communication. Increasingly, it also depends on electronic networks. As communication increases in speed and volume, organizations may be learning faster and becoming more responsive to their environment.

Pathologies of information flow include both too much information of the wrong kind and too little information about vital matters. The system must be designed and trained to filter information intelligently and in accordance with organizational needs. Responsibilities for the various critical processes of information processing must be carefully assigned. Important information must not fall into cracks in the system. On the other hand, although some redundancy is necessary, the principle of efficiency demands that duplication of effort in information processing be limited. Because inefficiencies in matter-energy processing tend to be more costly, however, it seems prudent to err on the side of too much rather than too little information flow.

Control by means of feedback has always been an important aspect of information flow in organizations. Recently, however, the emphasis has changed from controls that restore the status quo to controls that lead to continuous improvement. Feedback is used to diagnose process problems and improve the design of processes in accordance with broad organizational objectives. This sort of dynamic control process becomes the responsibility of everyone in the organization.

NOTES

1. Tom Peters, *Liberation Management: Necessary Disorganization for the Nanosecond Nineties* (New York: Knopf, 1992), 107–20.

2. James G. Miller, *Living Systems* (New York: McGraw-Hill, 1978), 22.

3. Ibid., 23.

4. Ibid., 23.

5. Ibid., 56, 609.

6. Ibid., 62, 623.

7. Ibid., 62, 625.

8. Ibid., 63–64, 627.

9. Jessie L. Miller, "The timer," *Behavioral Science* 35 (1990): 164.

10. Miller, *Living Systems*, 64, 635.

11. Ibid., 65, 637.

12. Ibid., 66, 639.

13. Ibid., 67, 642.

14. Ibid., 68–69, 662.

15. Ibid., 69, 664.

16. Richard L. Daft, Robert H. Lengel, and Linda K. Trevino, "Message equivocality, media selection, and manager performance: Implications for information sys-

tems," *MIS Quarterly* 11 (1987): 355–66.

17. Eliyahu M. Goldratt and Jeff Cox, *The Goal: A Process of Ongoing Improvement*, 2d ed. (Croton-on-Hudson, NY: North River, 1992).

18. W. Edwards Deming, *Out of the Crisis* (Cambridge, MA: MIT Center for Advanced Engineering Study, 1982), 18–96.

19. R. L. Flood, *Total Quality Management* (Hull, England: The University of Hull, 1990).

20. Peters, *Liberation Management,* 226–36.

21. Ibid., 3–19; Alvin Toffler, *The Adaptive Corporation* (New York: McGraw-Hill, 1985), 1–19.

22. Chris Argyris and D. A. Schon, *Organizational Learning: A Theory of Action Perspective* (Reading, MA: Addison-Wesley, 1978); Richard L. Daft and Karl E. Weick, "Toward a model of organizations as interpretation systems," *Academy of Management Review* 9 (1984): 284–95.

23. Peters, *Liberation Management,* 382–412.

24. Richard L. Daft and Robert H. Lengel, "Information richness: A new approach to managerial behavior and organization design," in Barry M. Staw and L. L. Cummings (Eds.), *Research in Organizational Behavior,* Vol. 6 (Greenwich, CT: JAI Press, 1984), 191–233.

25. Perception is functionally selective. See Hypothesis 3.3.3.2–20 in Miller, *Living Systems,* 97.

26. Henry Mintzberg, *The Structuring of Organizations* (Englewood Cliffs, NJ: Prentice-Hall, 1979), 431–67; Henry Mintzberg, "Organization design: Fashion or fit?" *Harvard Business Review* 59, no. 1 (1981): 103–16.

27. George P. Huber, *Managerial Decision Making* (Glenview, IL: Scott, Foresman, 1980); Andre L. Delbecq, Andrew H. Van de Ven, and David H. Gustafson, *Group Techniques for Program Planning: A Guide to Nominal Groups and Delphi Techniques* (Glenview, IL: Scott, Foresman, 1975); John Harmon and John Rohrbaugh, "Social judgment analysis and small group decision making: Cognitive feedback effects on individual and collective performance," *Organizational Behavior and Human Decision Processes* 46 (1990): 34–54.

28. Irving L. Janis, *Groupthink*, 2d ed. (Boston: Houghton Mifflin, 1982).

Chapter 6

Managing Matter-Energy Flow

One stage of the production process at NewVent has become a bottleneck, causing missed shipping deadlines and idle time at other stages. Terry doesn't usually deal with production problems, but the proposed solution to this one involves a large expenditure for additional automated machinery. Terry wonders whether additional machinery is really the answer, or whether it is simply a scheduling problem.

A major function of management is to see that products or services are delivered on time at a cost that is acceptable to the firm and the customer. One way to meet this responsibility may be to produce the output at minimum cost and hold it in inventory until needed. This is generally not possible with services, however, and increasingly manufacturers are minimizing inventory costs by producing to order. With proper scheduling of production stages backward from the agreed time of delivery and with sufficient capacity in the subsystems, goods can be produced to order in minimum time and at very reasonable cost. NewVent appears to be unable to do this because of insufficient capacity in one of the components of the production subsystem.

In this chapter we review the critical subsystems that process matter and energy. Coordination of these processes by the decider subsystem is also discussed. Issues of cost, efficiency, and effectiveness are examined. Pathologies of the matter-energy subsystems are noted and solutions are suggested.

MATTER-ENERGY PROCESSING SUBSYSTEMS

Living systems are constantly consuming material and energy, and acquiring new matter and energy to make up the deficit. They consume some material to generate energy and transform other material into "products." Less obviously, they also consume or exchange the matter of which they are composed, replacing it with new matter. We may look the same from year to year, but most of the atoms of which we are composed have changed. It is the pattern of those atoms, the system, that is retained.

Because acquisition, transformation, and disposal of matter and energy are so important, it is not surprising that living systems have developed a set of specialized subsystems for the purpose. In Chapter 2 we discussed the processes performed by these subsystems. Here we take a closer look at the subsystems themselves.

Subsystems that Process Both Matter-Energy and Information

Boundary. Although we already examined the boundary subsystem in Chapter 5, we noted then that it processes not only information but also matter-energy. That is, the boundary selectively admits or rejects inputs of matter and energy, as well as retaining or rejecting what is already in the system, in accordance with the system's needs.

The boundary subsystem in an organization consists of every member or group that comes in contact with the organization's environment. Ultimately that includes everyone, because people are mobile. Yet some members have much more external contact than others. The organizational roles of guards, purchasing agents, mail clerks, shipping and receiving clerks, receptionists, and personnel recruiters ensure that they will have major boundary responsibilities with respect to matter-energy.

It is vital for the protection of the organization that every member who regularly deals with the public understands the purposes and goals of the organization. Only then can they make informed decisions about what to reject and what to allow passage.

For example, salespeople must know the firm's policies with respect to credit, prices, special orders, after-market service, and a host of other matters. Purchasing agents must be similarly aware of the firm's needs with respect to quality, price, credit, delivery, and so forth. These people are on the front line. Any mistakes they make in selectivity will probably cost much more to clean up later.

Reproducer. The reproducer subsystem processes matter and energy when it actually puts together a new system. For instance, the reproducer subsystem of a fast-food franchise may include construction teams that are able to erect a new store in a week or less. The Virtual Realty network has a standby team of technicians ready to set up the video equipment in each new office. Staffing a new subsidiary involves recruiting people, that is, acquiring their physical presence and energy, as well as training them. The human resources department is a chief component of the reproducer for processing both matter-energy (i.e., people) and information (e.g., training).

Except for franchise operations, reproduction is seldom a full-time job in organizations. Various members of an organization can be assigned to the function as needed, so long as they fully understand the template of the organization or, at least, the part of it that they must reproduce.

Organizational reproduction is not nearly as precise as biological reproduction. Imprecise copying may be an advantage, however. It permits adaptation of the new organization to circumstances that are different from those faced by the parent(s).

The reproductive role of a manager is to ensure that reproduction is essentially accurate and faithful to the parent organization, while at the same time allowing the new organization to adapt readily to its environment.

Subsystems that Process Only Matter-Energy

Ingestor. The ingestor subsystem "brings matter-energy across the system boundary from the environment."[1] In an organization, this process is often carried out by the same members who screen inputs as part of the boundary process. For example, salespeople not only bring orders into the system, but also screen them for acceptability of the terms.

One form of input is new employees or members. At NewVent, such ingestion activities as employee orientation and issuance of special clothing and safety gear are carried out by the Human Resources Department, with some help from supervisors. Shipping and receiving clerks log in new materials. Guards and receptionists sign in visitors and usher them to the proper offices. Secretaries and mail room clerks open packages, routing them to the proper destinations. Although the ingestion process occurs in many parts of the organization, it is primarily associated with the Human Resources Department and the Materials Receiving Department. In another organization, these functions may be grouped differently, of course.

Artifacts play an important role in the ingestion process. Pipes and wires bring water, gas, and electricity into the system; meters monitor the flow. Incoming shipments are weighed on scales. Visitors or customers may be counted by a revolving gate. Cranes and forklifts may be used to move materials from trailers onto the receiving dock. Boxes are opened with crowbars and knives.

Distributor. The distributor subsystem carries matter-energy throughout the system to each component.[2] Both inputs from the environment and outputs of other subsystems are carried by the distributor. At NewVent, this process is highly mechanized. Cranes, conveyor belts, chutes, electric carts, forklifts, trucks, rolling bins, pneumatic tubes, pipes, and wires are components of the distributor. All NewVent employees may at times carry materials from one place to another, but messenger clerks and drivers specialize in this process.

In a large organization, this process may be organized and assigned primarily to one unit, such as a materials handling department. A multi-plant firm may transport materials and employees from one plant to another by means of a motor transport group, but this task is often dispersed to railroads, trucking firms, and airlines.

Converter. The converter subsystem changes certain inputs into forms more useful for the special processes of the system or its customers.[3] Conversion involves acts such as cutting, chopping, grinding, shredding, crushing, melting, cooling, separating, and purifying materials. Organizational examples of this process would include heating water into steam, cracking crude oil into gasoline and other petroleum products, separating metals from ore, removing pollutants from the air, cutting sheets of steel into blanks for bottle caps, milling grain into flour, cutting lumber into boards, shredding cabbage to make cole slaw, grinding beef into hamburger, and converting electric power into light. Artifacts involved in this process would include boilers, saws, knives, shredders, grinders, separators, filters, motors, and light bulbs.

Some organizations, such as MVR, do little conversion; the process is dispersed to other systems. Organizations may buy electric power, pre-ground flour, precut lumber, and purified chemicals from other organizations, rather than buying the raw materials and converting them. Other organizations, such as utilities and meat packers, are built around the conversion process. When a manufacturing firm does its own conversion, the process is often organized into a group of its own, such as the boiler room or the cutting department.

Producer. The producer subsystem synthesizes materials and services. That is, it "forms stable associations that endure for significant periods among matter-energy inputs."[4] These inputs may first go through the converter. Production differs from conversion in that the producer builds and combines materials, whereas the converter breaks down and separates them or changes them into energy. The output of the producer may be intended for export to other systems or it may be used within the system for growth, repair of damage, or replacement of components. For instance, a machine shop usually makes parts for its own use as well as for sale.

Production is seen as the primary process of many organizations. For example, NewVent combines raw materials and energy into magnetic flanges. MVR links properties with customers. Restaurants combine raw foodstuffs into palatable meals. Publishers build paper, ink, and manuscripts into books and journals. A janitorial firm puts human energy and skill together to provide a service.

Figure 6-1
Buffering of the Central Production Core

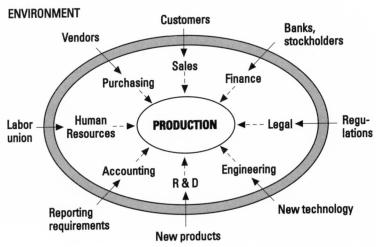

Because of its importance, the producer subsystem in organizations is often buffered from the environment.[5] As shown in Figure 6-1, departments such as sales, purchasing, engineering, and human resources stand between the production department and such elements of the environment as customers, suppliers, new technology, and the labor market. These buffers protect the producer subsystem from environmental stressors and allow the production process to proceed smoothly and efficiently. Thus, buffer departments act like a boundary for the producer subsystem.

Selling is also a producer process. It consists of forming a stable association between a product or service and a customer. Selling is the primary purpose of some organizations such as wholesalers, retailers, and realtors. In other organizations, this activity may be assigned to a separate sales department.

In many organizations, there are more people involved in the producer process than in any other critical process. Firms in labor-intensive industries may assign the majority of employees to roles in production. Most employees in retail sales organizations are directly involved in producing the sale. In organizations such as book publishers or research and development labs, however, part or all of the producer process is dispersed outward to subcontractors, vendors of parts and subassemblies, wholesalers, and retailers.

Artifacts of the producer include mixing vats, molds, stamping and printing machines, packaging and bottling machines, staplers, hammers, looms, sewing machines, paving machines, pots and pans, coffee urns, ovens, and display racks. In organizations that focus on production or sales, the producer subsystem is likely to include more artifacts than any other subsystem.

Management plays an important role in articulating the connection between converter and producer subsystems. It is becoming increasingly common for industrial firms to specialize in conversion or production, dispersing functions that are not regarded as central to the firm. Even specific stages of the production process may be subcontracted, with the firm retaining only what it regards as the technological core of its producer process. When this happens, it is very important for managers to form reliable links with other firms as vendors or customers for converted material and energy or for subassemblies.

Many firms are finding that, rather than playing vendors or customers off against each other in search of the best price, it pays to form a long-term alliance that focuses on quality, price, and service.[6] A single vendor with a long-term contract may be able to offer lower cost *and* better quality than any of the competitors for a short-term order could.

Storage. The storage subsystem retains deposits of various sorts of matter and energy within the system. Three stages are involved: (1) putting into storage, (2) maintenance, and (3) retrieving from storage.[7] For instance, inventory is (1) logged, tagged, and put on shelves; (2) periodically counted, checked, cleaned, and rotated; and (3) found and put into use when needed.

All members of an organization are likely to be involved at least occasionally in the storage and retrieval of items, but the storage process in organizations is primarily carried out by artifacts such as storage buildings, rooms, shelves, bins, pallets, racks, tanks, cabinets, file folders, drawers, and pockets. At NewVent, the storage of raw materials, parts, subassemblies, and finished products is assigned to the Inventory Department. Storage of energy resources such as electricity and natural gas is dispersed to other organizations.

As we noted in Chapter 4, storage of resources is a source of both cost and power. Good management can result in substantial savings in storage expenses. NewVent, for instance, has initiated a just-in-time (JIT) and *Kanban* production system that decreases the amount of materials stored in the system and thereby substantially reduces inventory costs.[8] (It should be noted that, unless NewVent's vendors can adopt a similar strategy, the storage costs may simply be dispersed to them.) The firm also uses algorithms for minimum reorder quantity and computer programs that automatically reorder based on sales entries.

Reduction of inventory costs may be good for the firm, but managers should consider the effects of inventory reduction on risk and power.

Less inventory may mean greater risk of lost sales if something uncontrollable occurs, such as breakdown of a critical machine, a work stoppage, or loss of a vendor. (It may also mean *less* risk of loss to fire or flood, of course.) Smaller inventories may also leave you at the mercy of key vendors or labor leaders, who see that your power is reduced. That is why a firm wishing to employ a JIT production strategy must have good relationships with vendors and labor, as well as close ties to its customers.

Extruder. The extruder subsystem "transmits matter-energy out of the system in the forms of products or wastes."[9] It completes the input-transformation-output cycle of the open system.

Extrusion involves finding either empty space in the nonliving environment or a living system that is willing and able to accept the organization's output. Making that output useful and attractive to other living systems is the basic goal of a firm's converter and producer processes. But these processes also generate waste matter and energy, which must likewise be expelled. The only real difference between products and wastes lies in their value to other living systems. Even garbage may have product value to recyclers and pig farmers.

The extrusion process in organizations is often carried out by specific groups or departments, such as a shipping department or a waste disposal crew. Artifacts involved in this process include loading docks, forklifts, trucks, railway cars, barrels, boxes, bags, tanks, pipes, smokestacks, and blowers. In retail sales organizations, the removal of merchandise and customers from the system is aided by paper sacks, shopping carts, chutes and conveyor belts, and trucks. The process may be partly dispersed to a package delivery firm.

A special kind of extrusion in business organizations is the daily exodus of employees to their homes. The process is aided by punch clocks, whistles, gates, and roads. Employees are "stored" in their homes during nonworking hours and retrieved for work by means of a daily process of input transduction.

Motor. The motor subsystem moves the system or parts of it in relation to its environment, or moves components of its environment in relation to each other.[10] This subsystem may include components such as a fleet of cars that carry sales representatives as they visit customers, trucks that transport materials from one firm to another, and shovels that move ore from one place to another. When a new subsidiary is being staffed, the motor subsystem may work in conjunction with the reproducer to move employees, their families, and their household goods to a new location.

Some organizations, such as railroads, airlines, steamship lines, and trucking firms, specialize in providing motor processes to other living systems. In organizations that have their own motor subsystems, the process may be carried out by a group such as the transport department or motor pool. A passenger steamship or an army is, in effect, an organization that moves itself with the aid of artifacts.

Major parts of the distribution, extrusion, and motor processes are often combined in a single group, such as a logistics department. Management of these processes can be critical to the success of the organization. Many firms have found that proper management of logistics can save substantial amounts of money and time, as well as improving customer satisfaction.

Supporter. The supporter subsystem maintains a proper spatial relationship among components of the system.[11] In organizations the supporter process is carried out almost entirely by artifacts. Buildings, floors, offices, dividers, chairs, desks, and vehicles are all part of the supporter subsystem of the average organization. A buildings and grounds crew may be assigned the task of maintaining the supporter. Design and construction of supporter subsystems is usually dispersed to other systems such as architectural firms and builders, or to owners from which buildings are leased.

Table 6-1 summarizes the organizational structures and artifacts commonly associated with the matter-energy processing subsystems, as well as systems to which these subsystems are sometimes dispersed.

COORDINATION OF CRITICAL SUBSYSTEMS

Although the processes of the twenty critical subsystems are separable, the subsystems do not act independently. Their activities are coordinated by the template and the decider subsystem. Thus, in discussing subsystems that process matter-energy, we cannot ignore their interaction with the information-processing subsystems.

Both sets of subsystems coexist in every living component of an organization. For example, the production department may be primarily organized around the producer process, but its members inevitably are also involved in information input and output, decoding and encoding, and the memory, associator, and decider processes. In fact, the interaction among processes is so great that it has led at least one group of theorists to devise a different set of subsystems organized around the concept of purpose and combining matter-energy and information processes.[12]

Table 6-1
Matter-Energy Processing Subsystems, Structures, Artifacts

Subsystem	Department or Group	Dispersed to:	Artifacts
Reproducer	Board of Directors overseas operations	legal firm construction firm	buildings equipment
Boundary	Security Department secretaries	police credit bureau	fence, gate alarms
Ingestor	Personnel Department Materials Receiving	specific members	pipes, wires cranes
Distributor	Materials Handling drivers, clerks	trucking firms airlines, railroads	pipes, wires forklifts
Converter	Boiler room cutters, grinders	utilities oil and chemical firms	saws, knives air filters
Producer	Production Department Sales Department	subcontractors wholesalers	staplers ovens
Storage	Inventory Department secretaries, clerks	utilities, suppliers warehousers	shelves parking lot
Extruder	Shipping Department waste disposal crew	city sanitation dept. each member	boxes, drums smokestack
Motor	Transport Department drivers	trucking firms mass transit	automobiles trucks
Supporter	Building and Grounds	leasing agents	buildings vehicles

Source: Lane Tracy, "Design for organizational health," *Journal of Business Research* no. 12 (1992), 19. Used by permission of the Research Institute Administration Office, College of Economics, Nihon University, Tokyo, Japan.

Management, or leadership, is what we call the decider process by which the activities of all other critical subsystems are coordinated. All of the chapters of this book are about some aspect of management and Chapter 9 especially focuses on problems of leadership, but here we are specifically concerned with coordination of matter-energy processes.

Optimization and Suboptimization

The critical matter-energy subsystems must be treated as part of a system, not as separate functions. Consequently:

Managers should not concentrate on optimizing one process, such as production, without considering the effects on other processes. To the degree that optimization is possible, it should be aimed at the effectiveness of the system as a whole, or at the very least the full set of matter-energy processing subsystems.

At several points I have mentioned total quality management (TQM) or Deming's principles of management because, of all the approaches I have seen, these come closest to encompassing the full set of matter-energy processes. Deming repeatedly points out how traditional production management suboptimizes by focusing on efficiency of production while ignoring the quality of inputs and outputs, costs of storage, speed of distribution, and other important factors.[13] Flood goes even further to encompass people factors and environmental interactions.[14]

Customer Satisfaction

What really counts, as an overall indicator of success for most business firms, is customer satisfaction. If a firm can satisfy its customers and still make a profit, it will survive in the short run. On the other hand, a firm that fails to satisfy its customers, or fails to make a profit while satisfying them, will quickly succumb. Yet, in order to satisfy customers, management must emphasize quality throughout the set of matter-energy processes.[15] That is, inputs must be of good quality, they must be handled properly in the distribution process, conversion and production must be carried out with quality in mind, and expulsion must be timely. Quality in this context means "what the customer wants."

Satisfaction, as we saw in Chapter 3, is never permanent. Indeed, satisfaction often leads to heightened aspirations. Today's satisfied customer may yearn for something even better tomorrow. Thus, Deming and other writers, such as Feigenbaum and Flood, have emphasized the importance of continual striving for improvement.[16] The methods they recommend are centered around employee participation and involvement at all stages, from the design of the product or service to actual delivery and beyond. In this scheme of things, management's role is to lead and coordinate the push for continuous improvement. This view of the manager's role receives further discussion in Chapter 10.

Despite the importance of quality and continuous improvement, management cannot lose sight of costs. Other firms may be competing for the same business, and they, too, may be able to produce high quality. When competition arises, the firm that combines quality and continuous improvement with efficiency will be the winner. Obviously, this is a tall order. It will not be met by managers who focus on *static* efficiency. What is needed is a push for dynamic efficiency.

Dynamic Efficiency

Efficiency was defined in Chapter 4 as the ratio of a system's success to the costs involved. Here we treat success in terms of creating output that has worth to other systems. Thus, efficiency is simply the ratio of the worth of output to the costs of output. That is,

$$\text{efficiency} = \frac{\text{worth of output}}{\text{costs of output}}$$

As a ratio, efficiency depends on both the numerator and the denominator. That is, efficiency can be increased by increasing the numerator or decreasing the denominator. Unfortunately, many managers focus almost exclusively on cost reduction.

How is the worth of output determined? Unless the organization is producing something for internal consumption, we are not talking about the worth of output *to the organization*. We mean the worth of output *in the marketplace* or *to a specific customer*. Thus, we are talking again about customer satisfaction. Cost, on the other hand, is determined by the values of the producing organization.

Both worth and costs are constantly changing. We have already noted that customer satisfaction may decrease even with no change in the product or service, simply because aspirations increase. Customers may also become satiated with a given product or service and be motivated to move on to something else.

Costs, meanwhile, may vary both with external change and with internal shifts in values. The price of various inputs may rise or fall with market fluctuations, of course. Also, the organization may find ways to reduce waste and make do with less resources. Yet costs change even with no shift in external costs or consumption. For instance, the values of workers in many parts of the world have moved toward according greater worth to autonomy, meaningful work, pleasant working conditions, and participation in decision making. Managers who ignore such shifts in values are unwittingly increasing the costs of output.

Management for dynamic efficiency, then, means balancing the worth and cost of outputs in an environment of changing values. Concern for quality is aimed at increasing the numerator, whereas concern for employee satisfaction and waste reduction is aimed at decreasing the denominator. Furthermore, these concerns interact. Increasing employee involvement in decision making, for instance, may simultaneously increase employee satisfaction (i.e., reduce psychic energy cost), reduce waste through closer attention to process, and increase customer satisfaction through better quality. Of course, if a manager's satisfaction is tied up in being the one to exercise authority and solve all problems, then this solution may be seen as having high cost for the manager.

Effectiveness

Concern for efficiency, even dynamic efficiency, should not cause us to forget that the organization must also be effective. That is, it must accomplish its purposes and goals. Customer satisfaction is an important goal and cost reduction is a vital purpose, but organizations have other goals and purposes as well.

An organization serves itself by fulfilling its purposes, as defined by its template. Such purposes for a business firm typically include positive cash flow, a certain level of profit after taxes, capital appreciation, growth of sales volume, maintenance or increase of value added per employee, optimum use of productive resources, and greater return on investment. Increased efficiency may contribute to fulfillment of many of these purposes, but it is not the only important variable. Indeed, in the short run a firm may willingly sacrifice some efficiency for faster growth, for instance.

With respect to goals an organization serves several constituencies or *stakeholders*, each of which has its own set of values. The stockholders of a firm may be primarily concerned with return on investment or capital appreciation. "Worth of output" is defined for them by the current stock price and their costs are set by the base price at time of purchase. Creditors may be satisfied with prompt payment of debts and a high credit rating. Employees are likely to be looking for high wages or salaries, good benefits, job security, job satisfaction, and a well-funded pension plan. Vendors might desire a long-term contract at a profitable price. The community may value continued employment opportunities, proper care for the environment, and tax revenues. Customers tend to measure the organization's effectiveness in terms of quality of output, price, and service.

Other constituencies may include various government bodies, labor unions, parent organizations, and subsidiaries. Each stakeholder has its own ways of measuring the effectiveness of the organization. An objective measurement of organizational effectiveness must take into account all of these viewpoints, albeit to varying degrees.[17]

As we discussed in Chapter 1, owners and managers differ in their willingness to accord legitimacy to the views of various stakeholder groups. Some owners and managers tend to exclude the concerns of hourly paid employees from consideration; others pay little attention to the values of customers or vendors; and many probably view government concerns as a threat rather than a legitimate measure of organizational effectiveness. Nonetheless, from a living systems viewpoint, the success of a system depends on its interaction with its environment.

The point of the stakeholder concept is that these elements of the organization and its environment perceive that they hold a stake in the success of the organization. Stakeholders measure the effectiveness of the organization by their standards, whether or not the owners or managers of the organization accord any legitimacy to those measurements.

Managers should at least be aware of how others measure the effectiveness of the organization. Other systems will act on those views and their actions will impact the organization.

PATHOLOGIES OF MATTER-ENERGY PROCESSING SUBSYSTEMS

The critical subsystems that process matter and energy may fail in a number of ways, some of which have already been suggested. Although the following list is far from complete, it sums up several pathologies commonly found in organizations, lists usual symptoms, and suggests treatments.

1. The boundary fails to exclude substandard materials and subassemblies, incompetent or disloyal employees, or substandard machinery; it fails to retain valuable employees, tools, and resources. Symptoms: frequent breakdown of machinery, frequent and costly rework, high scrap rates, high rates of absenteeism and turnover, lack of internal candidates for promotion, high rates of "shrinkage." Treatments: Specify clear standards for inputs. Train employees who must make input decisions. Be more careful and thorough in hiring procedures. Strengthen security. (But the best security comes from employees who are committed to the purposes and goals of the organization. For this you must reward desired behavior and build a strong company culture.) Gather information on the local labor market and try to match the wages, benefits, and working conditions offered by other employers.
2. Inefficient processes of ingestion, conversion, production, or extrusion. Symptoms: excessive waste and scrap, excessive pollution, poor quality output, delays in output, high cost. Treatments: First, identify the location(s) and source(s) of the problem. They may lie in poor planning and design, outmoded or poorly maintained machinery, poorly trained workers, low morale, overcontrol of processes, excessive overhead, unnecessary layers of management, or

all of the above. Second, try to treat causes rather than symptoms. Third, try to treat the problems as a system. Trying to deal with one cause at a time often doesn't work. A combination of treatments may be necessary.

3. Poorly managed storage. Symptoms: several years' supply of some items, backorders on others; many obsolete items in inventory; "lost" items—they show up on the records but cannot be located when needed; unrecorded items—they sit on the shelves but no one knows they are there; stored items deteriorating rapidly. Treatments: Decide that storage is important. Use coding, including color codes, to make problems more visible. Train employees; get them to help design the system. Installing a computerized inventory system will help, if it is well planned. Make sure that the system includes regular rotation and maintenance of stored items. Develop facilities for items that require special conditions.

4. Bottlenecks in the production process—this is the problem Terry faced at NewVent. Symptoms: some work stations are frequently idle, whereas others scramble to keep up; large piles of unfinished work in front of some stations; frequent use of expediters to handle late orders. Treatments: Identify the bottlenecks. Look for alternative ways to process materials—perhaps other machines can do the same job, even if less efficiently. Stop using expediters; they only create more problems. Instead, establish priorities and train employees to recognize and adhere to them. Buy additional machinery of the kind creating the bottleneck. Recognize that the cost of *not* resolving bottlenecks may be greater than the firm can afford.[18]

5. Dissatisfied customers. Symptoms: frequent complaints about price, quality, or service; requests for products you don't have; inability to meet promised delivery dates; cancelled orders; lack of repeat orders. Treatments: This problem is very serious and may indicate other problems in the organization. The traditional treatment might be to increase the advertising budget, hire more salespeople, expand the distribution territory, or make cosmetic changes in products. A more systemic treatment would begin by asking customers, including former customers, what they want. Then study the firm's capability for producing it. If it can't be done readily with your current system, it is time for a thorough shakeup. Try to get all of the employees involved, because the problem and its solution are multifaceted. If the firm can produce what the customer wants with its current system, of course, start doing so.

SUMMARY

Subsystems that process matter-energy are at the heart of many business firms. Even service-oriented firms and voluntary organizations must do some matter-energy processing. Effective management of the flow of matter and energy through the organization is important to its continued health and success.

Although we can separate the various critical processes conceptually, in reality each component unit of an organization usually is involved in several different processes. Primary coordination of these processes therefore occurs within the component. For instance, a production worker or work group may also be involved in distribution, conversion, storage, and decision making about the sequencing of these activities. Extracting the decision-making responsibility and assigning it to a manager would introduce delays, inefficiencies, communication errors and, quite possibly, a loss of work motivation in the worker(s).

The point of categorizing and describing the critical subsystems is not that they should be separated in fact, but that managers or leaders should be aware of the importance of all the critical processes. Managers should know where in the system these processes are occurring. This knowledge will aid them in the diagnosis and treatment of organizational problems.

Management should aim at optimization, or at least improvement, at the level of the whole organization, not each separate function. Efficiency of processes is important, but concern for efficiency can easily lead to suboptimization at the subsystem level. The use of dynamic efficiency as a criterion will help to avoid this pitfall.

For business firms, customer satisfaction serves as a good proxy variable for judging the effectiveness of the system as a whole. A broader view of organizational effectiveness can be obtained by including the assessments of other stakeholders, such as employees, vendors, stockholders, and the local community.

NOTES

1. James G. Miller, *Living Systems* (New York: McGraw-Hill, 1978), 57, 611.

2. Ibid., 57, 613.

3. Ibid., 57, 616.

4. Ibid., 58, 616.

5. James D. Thompson, *Organizations in Action* (New York: McGraw-Hill, 1967), 20–21.

6. W. Edwards Deming, *Out of the Crisis* (Cambridge, MA: MIT Center for Advanced Engineering Study, 1982), 35–40.

7. Miller, *Living Systems*, 58, 619–21.

8. Y. Sugimori, K. Kusunoki, F. Cho, and S. Uchikawa, "Toyota production sys-

tem and Kanban system materialization of just-in-time and respect-for-human system," *International Journal of Production Research* 15, no. 6 (1977): 553–56.

9. Miller, *Living Systems*, 59, 621.

10. Ibid., 59, 622.

11. Ibid., 60, 623.

12. Gyorgy G. Jaros and Anacreon Cloete, "Biomatrix: The web of life," *World Futures* 23 (1987): 203–24.

13. Deming, *Out of the Crisis*, 97–148.

14. Robert L. Flood, *Total Quality Management* (Hull, England: The University of Hull, 1990).

15. Philip B. Crosby, *Quality is Free* (New York: Mentor, 1980); Philip B. Crosby, *Quality without Tears* (New York: McGraw-Hill, 1984); J. M. Juran, *Juran on Planning for Quality* (New York: Free Press, 1988).

16. A. V. Feigenbaum, *Total Quality Control* (New York: McGraw-Hill, 1983); Flood, *Total Quality Management*.

17. Terry Connolly, Edward J. Conlon, and Stuart J. Deutsch, "Organizational effectiveness: A multiple-constituency approach," *Academy of Management Review* 5 (1980): 211–17; Michael Keely, "A social-justice approach to organizational evaluation," *Administrative Science Quarterly* 23 (1978): 272–92.

18. Eliyahu M. Goldratt and Jeff Cox, *The Goal: A Process of Ongoing Improvement*: 2d ed. (Croton-on-Hudson, NY: North River, 1992).

Chapter 7

Managing Internal Conflict and Stress

The Virtual Realty network is in the midst of an argument about fees for equipment maintenance. The franchise agreement indicates that the network will supply and maintain the special equipment needed for presentations to potential buyers. As the equipment has become more readily available, however, several agencies have discovered that they can obtain the equipment more cheaply from local suppliers. Furthermore, local maintenance and repair is quicker and less expensive in some locations.

Some of the larger agencies are pressing for a revision of the agreement either to reduce the equipment fees in line with the market or to allow local purchase and maintenance of the equipment. Agencies in smaller locations, although they wouldn't mind a reduction in fees, are happy with the current agreement. They do not want the conflict to escalate into a costly legal battle. Network headquarters thinks that the law is on its side and sees no reason to budge.

CONFLICT IN ORGANIZATIONS

Conflict is a fact of life for organizations. Business firms, for example, are in frequent conflict with each other over the cost, quality, and delivery schedule of goods and services, over market share, about patent infringement, and many other matters. Firms may also be in conflict with government regulatory agencies, labor unions, and citizens' watchdog groups concerning issues such as pollution of the environment, product safety, and treatment of employees. Banks, creditors, and stockholders may be in conflict with the firm over dividends and executive salaries. The firm may also be in conflict with individual employees concerning pay equity, performance demands, and discipline. Internal conflicts between departments and among individual employees about matters such as goals and budgets also affect the firm.

A basic task of management is to control these myriad conflicts so that the affairs of the organization can be conducted in a reasonably orderly fashion. Yet controversy exists as to whether it is better to resolve conflict or to manage it. *Conflict resolution* implies that the goal is to make conflict disappear. *Conflict management,* on the other hand, requires only that disputes be reduced to a level that allows the parties to cooperate where necessary. They may continue to disagree, so long as they can work with one another.

Given that a certain amount of conflict is probably good for the organization because it stimulates creativity, I will focus on conflict management rather than resolution. The goal of conflict management is cooperation, which is more than the absence of conflict. *Cooperation* involves working together toward a common goal for mutual benefit.

In this chapter I first attempt to analyze conflict as a phenomenon of relationships between components of a living system. Understanding the nature of conflict is necessary before we can proceed to a discussion and comparison of various methods of conflict management. We then examine the management of conflict within an organization. Management of conflict between organizations is discussed in Chapter 8.

SOURCES OF CONFLICT

Miller defined conflict as a *strain* that occurs when a system is required to respond simultaneously to two or more commands that "are incompatible—because they cannot be done simultaneously or because doing one makes it impossible later to do the other."[1] New strains in a system affect the hierarchy of values and thereby motivate behavior to relieve them (see Chapter 3). A strain that cannot be relieved causes *distress* or what is commonly but inaccurately called "stress."

Miller's definition of conflict might seem unduly restrictive, as it allows conflict to occur only *within* a system. We are used to thinking of conflict *between* systems, such as conflict between two firms or between a manager and subordinate. However, the effects of conflict occur within the conflicting parties. Furthermore, any two systems may be considered as a *dyad* (i.e., as a system in its own right) and the conflict can be analyzed as a phenomenon of the dyad. Systems that lack sufficient ongoing interaction to be considered a dyad cannot have any meaningful conflict.

Conflict can only be resolved or managed with respect to the values of a particular system. That is, the system determines the standards by which the solution is judged. When two firms negotiate an agreement to end a dispute, each firm must decide whether the agreement sufficiently relieves the strain it feels.

Note that conflict may be generated within a system by a command from another party that is incompatible with an *internal* command of the system. For instance, an organization may receive an order from a customer that cannot be met without disturbing an already established production schedule. Another example would be a manager receiving an order to carry out a transaction that she regards as unethical.

Conflict is usually treated as a phenomenon occurring at a specific system level, such as interpersonal or intergroup conflict. The living systems approach, however, permits development of a generic view of conflict as a result of interactions between systems at any level. This approach possesses the advantages of (1) enabling comparison of views of conflict at the various specific levels and (2) facilitating understanding of interlevel conflict, as between an organization and a member.

Conflict-Generating Characteristics of Living Systems

The basic sources of conflict, and of cooperation as well, lie in the characteristics of living systems. With respect to conflict and cooperation between systems, the important characteristics are

1. Living systems are open systems *interacting with the environment*, including other living systems.[2]
2. The behavior of living systems is *purposeful*; it is directed at fulfilling needs.[3]
3. Living systems *require inputs* of matter-energy and information, and they must rid themselves of excess products and wastes.
4. Every living system has a *hierarchy of values*, which is determined by its template and modified by learning.[4]
5. Living systems can exist only within *narrowly limited environmental conditions*; they may act on the environment (again including other living systems) in order to maintain or improve those conditions.
6. Living systems at all levels above the cell are composed largely of living systems at the next lower level. These lower-level systems have *defined roles* as components of the given suprasystem.

Conditions of Conflict

These six characteristics of living systems establish the basis for conflict by determining conditions that are likely to generate incompatible commands. Several different conditions of conflict may arise.

Resource conflict. The need for inputs, purposeful behavior, and interaction with the environment often result in resource conflict. When two or more individuals, groups, organizations, communities, or nations covet the same resources and those resources are insufficient to meet all needs, the systems are likely to issue and receive incompatible commands regarding the distribution of those resources.

Overt manifestations of resource conflict within an organization include competition between departments for capital resources and key personnel. Individual members vie for choice positions and offices.

Environmental conflict. Similarly, a system's needs for certain environmental conditions, combined with purposeful behavior and interaction with other systems, result in environmental conflict. When two or more individuals or social systems share the same environment but require different conditions, they are likely to issue and receive incompatible commands for action on the environment.

Environmental conflict is characterized within organizations by disputes over lighting, heating, cooling, and smoking. Subtler aspects of the work environment such as time pressure and sexual harassment may also generate environmental conflict.

Resource and environmental conflicts are strains engendered jointly in two or more systems by incompatibility of each system's own purposes and goals with those of other systems. Other forms of conflict are usually analyzed as if they affect only one system. One of these is conflict over the defined role.

Role conflict. Social systems issue commands defining roles for components. This may result in one of three types of role conflict:

1. Role sender conflict. Because of lack of coordination between role senders, they may issue commands to a role receiver that are incompatible with each other. An example would be a manager being ordered by her boss to produce a report by tomorrow and by the vice president of marketing to fly to Bogota immediately.
2. Role/value conflict. Role commands from a single sender may conflict with values of the receiver. For example, a manager may ask an hourly paid employee to work overtime without pay. The employee may regard this as unfair.
3. Loyalty conflict. Incompatible role commands may be issued by two or more systems in which the recipient has a role. An example is the conflict generated within a sales manager who is asked to put on his corporate hat when he sits in a planning meeting as representative of his department. This form of conflict is discussed further in Chapter 9.

Role conflict has been studied extensively, although not from a systems point of view.[5] Research on role conflict has been mostly concerned with its effects on the individual, rather than on the organization.

Value conflict. Finally, the hierarchy of values may engender conflict within a living system. A living system's hierarchy of values is constantly changing and may not be internally consistent. Lack of consistency may result in generation of incompatible commands for action by the system, as when the ego calls for aggressive action but the superego advises caution.

Value conflict manifests itself in the form of inconsistent or unpredictable behavior, difficulty in making decisions, and, in extreme cases, paralysis. An organization fraught with value conflict may delay action until it is too late or may behave erratically, changing course from day to day.

METHODS OF CONFLICT MANAGEMENT

There are several basic ways in which conflict is managed. The most elemental, perhaps, is *domination*. For example, a manager may try to use coercive power to force employees or departments to stop fighting each other.

Domination often works well with subordinate systems. By threatening reprisals, a manager can impose a solution on two subordinates who are fighting over job assignments. An employer can often force individual employees to accept whatever wage it chooses to offer. But domination does not work well with systems of relatively equal power.

Influence is a subtle form of domination. Influence usually relies on the application of one or more of the bases of power discussed in Chapter 4. By promising rewards, claiming superior knowledge, or exerting charisma, a manager may be able to convince others to accept a particular solution to a conflict. Even though no force is used, this is still domination because it results in resolution of the conflict on the manager's own terms.

Authority is a particular source of influence that may be used to manage conflict. Authority is based on the subordinates' acceptance of the legitimacy of a command. Legitimacy may come from the fact that the person who is exercising authority is assumed to be acting on behalf of a suprasystem to which they all belong. For instance, disputing divisions of a large corporation may accept a settlement dictated by corporate headquarters. Subordinates may accept the authority of their boss to order them to suppress their personality differences in the interests of the firm. When authority works properly, other sources of power such as rewards and punishments are unnecessary.

Management of conflict by means of authority is complicated by the fact that managers who are attempting to resolve a dispute are often parties to it. They are tempted, therefore, to exercise authority to suppress conflicts or resolve them in their own favor. Yet often the firm would be better off in the long run if conflicts were managed in some other manner.

Persuasion is a particularly subtle form of domination. Its aim is still to resolve a dispute on the terms of the persuader, but without the expenditure of any resources. Instead, the persuader relies on the susceptibility of the conflicting parties to logic, innuendo, flattery, repetition, and other forms of persuasive rhetoric. For instance, one manager may persuade another to drop a claim for compensation by convincing the other manager that he will be seen as a better person for it.

When one system cannot dominate another on its own, it may seek a *coalition* with other systems in order to increase its power. Department heads form coalitions to influence budget decisions. Employees band together in a labor union to bargain for wages. Of course, the coalition itself involves exchange with other systems, such as promises of aid between department heads. But each member of the coalition may gain more from the exercise of collective power than it gives up to other members.

Parties who cannot resolve a conflict by themselves may also appeal to a third party for a decision. *Arbitration* and *adjudication* are common forms of third-party conflict management. Both processes invest authority in the third party to settle the dispute according to law, precedent, or common sense.

A manager who cannot dominate a relationship may choose to avoid it. Thus, *avoidance* is another method of managing conflict. Two managers who are involved in a dispute may simply stay away from each other. Yet avoidance may be costly. Exchanges with other systems often offer the greatest opportunities for benefit. Other members of the organization may have power precisely because their work is so valuable or they are such valued clients.

Submission or *appeasement* is another way to manage conflict. If the issue is not particularly important to a manager, giving in may offer the advantages of a quick settlement and development of an obligation that can be called on in future conflict situations.

When power is relatively equal, the most common method of managing conflict is *negotiation*. This method receives special attention here because of its importance as a regulator of exchange relationships within the organization.

NEGOTIATION

Negotiation is a motivated process of communication between living systems with the goal of reaching agreement about certain joint or reciprocal acts. These acts may involve management of conflict, exchange of resources, or cooperation on actions directed at the mutual environment.

Behavior within a system is normally regulated by the template of that system. Internal conflict may indicate a need to amend the template. Negotiation can be used to modify the template so as to remove the source of conflict. For instance, when negotiation occurs between components or subsystems of a system, as in talks to manage conflict between two divisions of a corporation, the resulting agreement may modify the template with respect to the roles and required behavior of the divisions.

A Living Systems View

Living systems theory offers a view of the negotiation process that differs substantially from the picture provided by other approaches, such as those found in the fields of economics, political science, or communication theory. From a living systems perspective, negotiation is a partial merging of the decider subsystems of the participants. It is a merger because the outcome is a joint decision; it is partial because during the bargaining process the participants pursue their own purposes and goals as well as those of the joint enterprise.

It is not entirely novel to say that negotiation results in a joint decision. Gray wrote that "collaboration involves a process of joint decision making among key stakeholders of a problem about the future of that domain."[6] But living systems theory indicates that *all* negotiation, whether collaborative or competitive, involves joint decision making. Indeed, Gray's argument could be turned around to say that, because negotiation is joint decision making, most negotiations should be collaborative in order to maximize the joint benefits.

Joint decision making occurs because, under certain conditions, it is beneficial to organizations to act together rather than separately. Mutual benefit may accrue from several sources: economies of scale, shared interests, mutually preferred positions, and various differences in values that permit mutually satisfactory exchange. Thus, as Lax and Sebenius put it, negotiation is partly a process of creating worth for the participants.[7]

To create worth, negotiators must define joint or compatible goals, share information, jointly develop alternatives, and agree on the choice of acts. Yet negotiation is also a process of claiming, that is, partitioning the newly created worth and apportioning it to the participants. In this part of the process, the participants pursue their own goals, which are often incompatible with those of other participants. They withhold information, develop alternatives favoring their own interests, and try to persuade other participants to agree with their own preferred choice.

Negotiators, as representatives of the participating systems, are often caught in the middle of these conflicting aspects of the process. The negotiators are the primary components of the merged decider, but they are also components of the deciders of their respective parties. Thus, negotiators may be torn between pursuit of joint goals and separate goals, between sharing information and withholding it, between developing alternatives for mutual gain and for separate gain, and between choosing the optimal joint outcome or the optimal selfish outcome.

Models of Negotiation

Many models of negotiation have been proposed, particularly for predicting the outcome of bargaining. These models come from a variety of fields of knowledge. An examination of the models proposed in even one field, such as labor relations, would (and does) fill a book. Thus, in this chapter I offer only limited comparisons with existing models.

Certain features are prominent in most, if not all, models of negotiation. For instance, negotiation obviously involves communication between the parties. Messages may be extensive, consisting of complex proposals, arguments for those proposals, arguments against the other party's position, and warnings of the consequences of failure to agree. Or the messages may be very limited, consisting only of tentative moves or statements of specific positions without explanation. Yet some amount of communication is necessary. In certain models, the communication process, itself, becomes the focus of analysis.

Another feature of most models is iteration or "rounds." Negotiation usually involves a series of proposals and counterproposals, gradually moving toward a central range of positions that are acceptable to both (or all) parties. The proposals and counterproposals may be preprogrammed to some extent, but it is ordinarily assumed that they are also responsive to each other. That is, B's counterproposal depends on the substance and/or style of A's proposal.

Finally, most models are concerned with determinants of the final outcome. They seek to answer questions such as: How is agreement reached, or what causes an impasse? Given a range of outcomes acceptable to all parties, what determines which of these outcomes will actually be chosen? How can one party influence another in order to obtain an outcome that is preferable to others within the acceptable range? What is the effect of power on outcomes?

Other features of the process are less frequently modeled. For instance, there is relatively little concern for implementation of the agreement. Yet those who have looked at this feature have found that the way in which the process is conducted has substantial effects on how the agreement is carried out.[8] A negotiation that leaves one of the parties barely satisfied, while enriching the other party or parties, may be difficult to implement. The disgruntled party may find ways, in essence, to continue the negotiation by being uncooperative in carrying out the agreement. In labor relations, for example, a union that is forced to agree to wage and benefit reductions may file a large number of grievances, making it difficult to administer the labor contract.

Another aspect of negotiation that has only recently become the focus of concern is how the process can be shaped to lead to an improved or expanded set of outcomes. Traditional views of the negotiation process have taken the range of possible outcomes as a given. It is now recognized that the negotiation process may provide means to create worth for the parties, as well as coming to agreement about the apportioning of that benefit. In order to create worth, however, communications must become more open and must focus on interests rather than positions.[9] When these steps are taken, negotiation becomes, in part, a problem-solving process.

A basic assumption of all negotiation models is that the parties will be collectively better off with an agreement than without one. That is, the joint payoff is greater than the sum of separate payoffs to the negotiating systems if there were no agreement. But there is no assumption that each of the negotiating systems will individually be better off. A rational system might agree to cooperate with others if there is no net loss in doing so. Long-range considerations (e.g., development of an obligation) or the exertion of power by another system may, indeed, cause a system to agree to a negatively valued proposal.

The values of the negotiating parties ultimately determine the viability of any agreement. So long as the agreement continues to produce benefits or reduce liabilities for all of the participants, the agreed-on system of interaction is likely to continue. For example, a coalition of managers within NewVent seeking approval to develop a new application of the magnetic flange principle may remain stable so long as the proposal is still being considered, but it will probably dissolve if the idea is not approved.

A Living Systems Model

To develop a descriptive living systems model of the negotiation process, we must first recognize that bargaining involves an exchange of information between two or more living systems. To simplify the model I consider only the two-party case, but the model can be generalized to multiparty negotiations. For two cycles of the iterative process the exchange of information may be analyzed by employing the systems dyad, as shown in Figure 7-1.

Figure 7-1
Dyadic Negotiation System

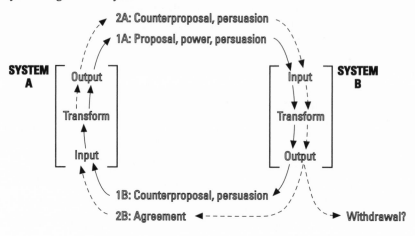

Round 1: ─────▶
Round 2: ─ ─ ─ ─▶

In the model, system A conveys a proposal to system B, expecting as a response either agreement to the proposal or a counterproposal. System A may also transmit power messages and arguments in favor of the proposal.

Figure 7-1 shows an iterative negotiation in which B offers a counterproposal in the first round but agrees to A's counterproposal in the second round. System B could also respond by refusing the proposal and withdrawing from negotiation. This would indicate that B sees no gain from agreement, even though A does.

The model is symmetric in that either A or B may initiate the process. There is no assumption that A and B are equal in status, power, or system level, however. One of the advantages of the living systems approach is that it can easily handle situations in which the parties are on different system levels, such as negotiation between a business firm and a government agency.

In many negotiations, the negotiators are acting as agents for other systems. An example would be two attorneys negotiating the dissolution of a marriage. The negotiators are bargaining not only with each other but also with their constituents. Often an agreement reached between the negotiators is less beneficial than their respective constituents expected; the negotiators must then bargain with their constituents to get them to accept the deal.

Another level of complexity occurs when the parties are represented by teams of negotiators rather than individual agents. Although it is typical to have one person, the chief negotiator or spokesperson, in charge of the team, that person must often negotiate with other team members concerning strategy, tactics, and positions to be taken.

If the negotiations are conducted by teams and the constituents are organizations, there may also be another level of negotiation going on within the hierarchy of these systems. For instance, there may be disagreement within the negotiating team, or a proposed agreement may be viewed more positively at some levels of the constituent hierarchy than at others. These differences of opinion must be resolved, often through negotiation, before the agreement can be ratified. An example would be negotiation at NewVent between Terry and the Director of Human Resources over ratification of the labor contract.

Major negotiations involving organizations, communities, and nations tend to fit this more complex, multilayered model. Yet such complexities may also arise in negotiations to resolve conflict within a business firm. A conflict on the shop floor between a production supervisor and a safety engineer concerning the workability of some new safety equipment may ultimately require interdepartmental negotiations at the vice presidential level or in a joint committee.

Practical Negotiating

The techniques and strategies of negotiation are equally relevant at several levels of living systems, as well as between levels, so long as power is relatively equal. Thus, the study of negotiation is interdisciplinary and is becoming a discipline in its own right.

The focus of study used to be on how to "win" at negotiation.[10] The current trend, however, is toward methods of collaborative negotiation in which the objectives are to obtain a more cooperative long-term relationship and a more rewarding substantive outcome for everyone. There are several good books on collaborative negotiation.[11] Nevertheless, I will offer here a few basic suggestions for managers:

1. *Recognize that relationships with most other living systems offer opportunities for mutual gain.*
2. *Treat negotiation as a means to explore these opportunities. Encourage the other party or parties to do likewise. Specifically,*
    a. *Be aware of the potential for negotiation to improve both the relationship and the substance of any exchanges between the systems. Treat the relationship and substantive exchanges as separate matters.*

    b. *Try to understand your own interests as well as those of the other party or parties. Express your interests instead of, or in addition to, your positions, and ask the others to do likewise.*

    c. *Invent options that may create mutual or joint gain. These may be packages of existing proposals or completely new ideas for exchange. Brainstorming may be useful in inventing options.*

    d. *Look for objective measures of a good outcome for both or all parties. One objective measure is your best alternative if the current negotiation fails. Be sure you know what that alternative is; develop it, if necessary. Other objective measures may involve precedents, principles of fairness, or the judgment of neutral observers.*

3. *Be well prepared. Preparedness is 90 percent of the battle in negotiation. Know what you want, what you have to offer, and the strategy and tactics you plan to use. Try to assess in advance what other systems want, what they have to offer, and what strategy and tactics they are likely to use. Know what you will do if negotiation does not succeed.*

STRESS

An input or output that forces system variables beyond their range of stability (see Chapter 3) constitutes *stress*.[12] Conflicting commands are one kind of stressful input, but there are many others.

Stress generates strain within the system. Ordinarily the system copes with strain by means of motivated behavior directed at changing the stressful input or output. Normal stress is no problem; in fact, it is called "eustress" and it motivates high performance.[13] If the system cannot cope, however, the result is *distress*. When stress results in symptoms of distress, something must be done about it before it harms people or destroys the organization.

Employees who are in distress may show a variety of symptoms. They may perform poorly or erratically. They may abuse drugs or alcohol, or engage in other forms of self-destructive behavior. They may show frantic bursts of energy followed by periods of depression.

Employees in distress need help from someone to relieve the stress, because they are unable to do so by themselves. If they get no relief, the result may be a heart attack or nervous breakdown.

Departments and even whole organizations may exhibit similar signs of distress. Typical symptoms are chaos, lack of cooperation, sabotage, backstabbing, frequent random changes of direction, and other forms of ineffective or destructive behavior. If stress remains unrelieved for long periods of time, the organization may collapse and dissolve.

Managers can often relieve stress and prevent distress at each level, but first they must recognize the symptoms. One way to do this is to observe normal system behavior and form a clear picture of it to serve as a baseline. When the behavior of an individual, department, or the organization departs from this baseline for an extended period, it is time to check the stresses on the system.

The kind of stress that leads to distress is one that causes an unrelievable strain. Reasons why the system cannot reduce the strain include lack of power, time, and ability. For example, an employee may never have the time to complete all of the tasks she is assigned, so that the work keeps piling up. A department may lack the resources to do its task well, resulting in constant dissatisfaction with its output.

Because the key to distress lies in the coping ability of the system, one person or department may suffer from a given level of stress while another thrives on it. That is why a manager needs a behavioral baseline for each system. Distress usually cannot be predicted simply by observing the *stressors* (i.e., the inputs and outputs) of the system. A generalized approach of reducing stress in the work environment is usually not effective. Besides, there are often unknown stressors from outside the work setting contributing to the problem. For instance, an employee's distress may be attributable more to conflict at home than to work pressures.

Having noted symptoms of distress and identified potential stressors, a manager may or may not be able to help. If some or all of the stressors are under managerial control, treatment can be relatively easy. For instance, an employee who is swamped with work can be given some temporary help or a lighter load. A department that is suffering from unrelieved conflict with another, more powerful department can be given added power so that it can negotiate a reasonable agreement.

When the stressors are not under managerial control, as when an employee's domestic situation is falling apart, it may not be wise to lighten the employee's work load. Maintaining a feeling of competence at work may be holding him together. Instead, help should focus on giving the employee skills to cope with the problem. The organization may offer or pay for family counseling services, alcoholism and drug abuse rehabilitation, psychological counseling, and training in problem solving as well as the usual range of medical services. The role of the manager may be to encourage use of these aids, because employees are often reluctant to admit that they need them.

SUMMARY

Living systems theory provides a framework for understanding conflict and its sources in the common characteristics of living systems. From this framework we were able to identify four distinct conditions of conflict: (1) mutually desired resources, (2) shared environment, (3) incompatible roles, and (4) inconsistent values.

One common thread running through our discussion of conflict management is the theme of power equalization. Roughly equal power encourages negotiation toward compromise or collaboration. Large power differentials stemming from subordination, or differences in size or level, encourage domination and appeasement. Ability to withdraw or avoid interaction, to form a coalition, or to appeal to a mediator or arbitrator may provide means for circumventing the power differential and enabling agreement on terms of interaction that are more mutually fulfilling.

Stress may be desirable or undesirable, depending on a system's ability to relieve the strains that it produces. A manager should learn to identify symptoms of distress in the organization and its components. In many cases, the manager can act to relieve distress, either by modifying stressors that are under managerial control or by helping victims to increase their ability to handle stressors.

NOTES

1. James G. Miller, *Living Systems* (New York: McGraw-Hill, 1978), 39.

2. Ibid., 18.

3. Lane Tracy, "Toward an improved need theory: In response to legitimate criticism," *Behavioral Science* 31 (1986): 211–12.

4. Miller, *Living Systems*, 39.

5. Robert L. Kahn, D. Wolfe, R. Quinn, J. Snoek, and R. Rosenthal, *Organizational Stress: Studies in Role Conflict and Ambiguity* (New York: Wiley, 1964); John R. Rizzo, Robert J. House, and Sidney I. Lirtzman, "Role conflict and ambiguity in complex organizations," *Administrative Science Quarterly* 15 (1970): 150–63.

6. Barbara Gray, *Collaborating: Finding Common Ground for Multiparty Problems* (New York: Jossey-Bass, 1989).

7. David A. Lax and James K. Sebenius, *The Manager as Negotiator: Bargaining for Cooperation and Competitive Gain* (New York: Free Press, 1986).

8. Ibid., 276–89.

9. Roger Fisher and William Ury, *Getting to Yes: Negotiating Agreement without Giving In*, 2d ed. (New York: Penguin, 1991).

10. Chester L. Karrass, *The Negotiating Game* (New York: Crowell, 1970).

11. Max H. Bazerman and Roy J. Lewicki (Eds.), *Negotiating in Organizations* (Beverly Hills: Sage, 1983); Fisher and Ury, *Getting to Yes*; Lax and Sebenius, *The Manager as Negotiator*; William Ury, *Getting Past No: Negotiating with Difficult People* (New York: Bantam, 1991).

12. Miller, *Living Systems*, 34.

13. Hans Selye, *Stress without Distress* (Philadelphia: J. B. Lippincott, 1974).

Chapter 8

Managing Environmental Relationships

Jan Garr, NewVent's Director of Employee Relations, has alerted Terry that NewVent may have labor problems. The Amalgamated Cryogenic Workers Union (ACWU) has presented signed authorization cards from 65 percent of the work force and petitioned for recognition. Official company policy, promulgated by UniGlobe, is that NewVent prefers to deal directly with its employees rather than through a union. Nevertheless, UniGlobe frowns on strong arm tactics to resist unions. It expects management to meet the needs of employees so that they will not want a union. Jan wants advice from Terry on how to handle the situation.

ORGANIZATION AND ENVIRONMENT

An organization must maintain relationships with various parts of its environment. Some of the most important environmental relationships are with other organizations. If the relationships are properly managed, these other organizations may be reliable sources of supply or regular customers. Having such relationships substantially reduces uncertainty for the organization and allows it to plan its operations for increased efficiency and effectiveness.

Even though an organization must remain open to its environment, it cannot be completely open. Its boundary subsystem must monitor the environment and reject potentially harmful inputs. It must also prevent the loss of valuable components and resources, unless the organization receives something of equal or greater worth in exchange.

Exchange is the key word. Most relationships with other systems involve exchange of resources. In order to succeed, an organization must engineer trades that increase the fulfillment of its own needs. Managers must make sure that exchange occurs on favorable terms.

This chapter discusses ways in which environmental relationships are managed. In particular, the role of negotiation again receives attention. Because the boundary subsystem is charged with the responsibility of controlling the interface between a system and its environment, we also review the boundary process.

REGULATING EXCHANGE BETWEEN SYSTEMS

In Chapter 4, we saw that organizations must constantly deal with other systems in order to obtain resources. Sometimes resources can be gained directly from nonliving systems or from living systems that are unable to offer effective resistance, such as forests and schools of fish. More often, however, resources are obtained through exchange with other organizations.

Interdependence

Cooperative exchange between living systems tends to form a new dyadic system, such as the one presented in Figure 8-1. This figure, which shows the exchange relationship between a firm and a customer, may be used to explain the concept of interdependence between systems.

Figure 8-1
Dyadic Relationship between Firm and Customer

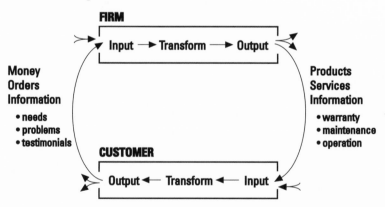

In addition to the exchange within the dyad, Figure 8-1 indicates that there are inputs from and outputs to other systems. The number of such alternative sources and recipients partly determines the degree to which each member of the dyad is dependent on the other. The amount and nature of resources they each require or have available, the degree to which one resource can be substituted for another, the storage capacity of each member, and the willingness and ability of each member to forego fulfillment of a need, if necessary, are other factors that determine the degree of interdependence.

If, as in the case of Cryorubber and NewVent, (1) the firm is the only available source of a resource required by the customer, (2) there are no suitable substitutes, (3) the customer has little storage capacity for the resource, and (4) is unable to do without it, then the customer is very dependent on the firm. The firm would have considerable power over the customer in such a circumstance; but the firm may have a similar dependence on something supplied by the customer. When the dependency is mutual, a strong bond is formed.

Very long lasting relationships may be built on mutually positive exchange between systems, even if the degree of interdependence is not high. If the exchange meets constantly recurring needs, a strong bond may be formed as a matter of convenience. Over time the terms of the exchange are codified and the bond becomes capable of replicating itself. When that happens, the dyad has become a living system.

Other, less permanent relationships, such as between buyer and seller or audience and performer, are also built on mutually beneficial exchange. The relationship may lack permanence because the needs that are met are evanescent or because there are many other systems offering similarly beneficial exchanges. Most dyads of living systems form and dissolve very easily.

Terms of Exchange

Dealings with other organizations often involve conflict over the terms of exchange. Thus, the various methods of resolving conflict, which we examined in Chapter 7, are again relevant to this discussion. For instance, one organization may attempt to dominate another to obtain what it wants. In the long run, the use of force by one organization on another usually results in retaliation, but domination often works well with non-living systems. The earth is unable to resist the power of dynamite, drills, and shovels. Even living systems such as forests can offer little resistance to axes, chain saws, and bulldozers.

Coalitions may also be useful in setting the terms of exchange. Two or more firms may combine forces to put together a bid on a complex project. Business firms also form coalitions to influence legislation or to resist foreign competition.

Influence is often useful. Although charisma is seldom a factor between organizations, rewards, punishments, expertise, and persuasion can often be brought to bear on other organizations in order to alter the terms of exchange in one's favor. NewVent, for instance, seeks to obtain favorable contracts from its customers on the basis of its acknowledged expertise in magnetic flange design.

Independent organizations cannot claim authority over each other. Nevertheless, they may employ the authority of a third party to settle disputes over terms of exchange. For instance, a business firm may call on the courts to enforce a patent or a contract with another firm, or the two firms may employ an arbitrator to settle the dispute.

Organizations may also agree to disagree, and simply avoid dealing with each other. Yet avoidance in the business world is often an expensive solution, because it gives up opportunities for potentially profitable trade. The very differences that make one organization want to avoid another may be the basis of mutually beneficial exchange.

Organizations need each other and they tend to be relatively equal in power. For these reasons negotiation is the most common and most useful method of regulating exchange between organizations. For instance, to obtain a favorable lease an organization discusses terms with one or more potential lessors until it reaches a mutually acceptable agreement with one of them.

Agreed Systems

The outcome of every negotiation between organizations, if it is successful, is an agreement that serves as the template for a new living system, which I call the *agreed system*. In administering the agreement, components of the decider subsystems of each member make decisions on behalf of the agreed system in accordance with its template, or else the agreement establishes a separate decider subsystem for the agreed system. Other critical subsystems of the agreed system may be dispersed to the member systems or elsewhere, although long-term agreements such as a merger accord may generate a more nearly totipotential system.

Some negotiations, for example plea bargaining or purchasing a building, produce agreements of such short duration that the existence of an agreed system is hardly noticeable. The agreed system may last only long enough to exchange money and property or perform required legal acts. Other negotiations produce an agreed system that combines and submerges the negotiating systems. An example would be negotiations leading to a merger of two corporations.

A complex negotiation may generate several agreed systems, corresponding to the many levels of bargaining. To illustrate, let us assume that the negotiation is between teams representing two corporations over development of a joint venture. The decider hierarchy of each corporation negotiates an internal agreement as to how it will act during the negotiations, what instructions it will give to its negotiating team, and how it will respond to various proposals from the other side. It then negotiates with its team of representatives to obtain agreement on how the team will act on behalf of the corporation. This provides a basic template for the team. Thus, each negotiating team is itself an agreed system.

Bargaining within the team then provides role instructions for each member. The teams bargain with each other to decide the terms under which the joint venture will operate. They are thus jointly designing the template of a new agreed system. In doing so they are acting as a partially merged decider subsystem.

Negotiation is a process by which the decider subsystems of two or more systems may be temporarily joined in order to make decisions concerning joint or reciprocal acts. Those acts constitute the behavior of the agreed system. In some cases, such as the prior example of negotiation of a joint venture, the agreed system is expected to continue for some time. For practical purposes this means that it will require a decider subsystem of its own. The template for the agreed system must then be elaborate enough to provide instructions for its decider subsystem and other subsystems.

Living systems models of the negotiation process (see Chapter 7) reveal that it is, in fact, part of the reproducer subsystem of each of the negotiating systems. The output of the process is often a template for a new living system. That system may be evanescent or long-lived. It may also be highly dependent on its parent systems or quite independent of them. Let us now look at the various kinds of agreed systems in more detail.

Kinds of Agreed Systems

Agreed systems vary greatly in duration and complexity. In some cases, they are so transitory that it is difficult to perceive their existence at all. In other cases, the whole point of the negotiations is to create a system that will endure.

The key to differences in agreed systems appears to lie in the goals of the negotiation. Negotiations may be intended (1) to resolve or manage conflict within systems, (2) to determine the terms of an exchange between systems, (3) to set up the conditions for continued cooperation between and among systems, or (4) to create a new system. In what sense is an agreed system generated by each of these types of negotiation?

Conflict management. When negotiation is used to resolve or manage conflict within a system, that system itself is the agreed system. The focus of negotiation is to amend that part of its template that governs the conflict. For instance, negotiation between two bickering partners may be aimed at altering the responsibilities of each partner. The agreement establishing the partnership already specifies role behaviors for the partners, but negotiation may be necessary to clarify or amend the agreement so that the partners can cooperate more effectively. Tasks may be redefined, rewards may be modified, and joint goals may be emphasized in order to reduce the conflict.

Terms of exchange. Negotiation to set the terms of an exchange, such as purchase of new machinery or acquisition of a business firm, usually creates a very temporary agreed system. The decider subsystem of the agreed system is simply the merged decider of the negotiators; the template is the oral or written contract. As soon as the agreed-on terms of the exchange are carried out, including any required legal processing, the agreed system ceases to exist.

Terms of continuing cooperation. Some forms of exchange, on the other hand, require a continuing agreed system. A purchasing contract for a steady supply of goods over a period of months or years, for instance, needs some sort of system to implement and monitor the exchange. It is usually not the negotiators who carry out these continuing processes of the agreed system. Rather, other agents of the contractual parties administer the agreement. But note that these agents are acting under the template established by the contract. Thus, they are temporarily performing as components of the agreed system.

A purchasing contract for a steady supply of goods is a simple example of the third type of agreed system, because it involves continued cooperation between the parties. More complex examples include labor contracts, service contracts between business firms, waste disposal agreements among communities, and treaties among nations for arms reduction, pollution control, and sharing of natural resources. In each case, an agreed system, such as a joint committee or inspection group, is set up. The agreed system cannot exist independent of the contractual parties. Instead, it relies on the services of components from the contractual parties acting under the template of the agreement.

A labor contract, for example, requires that the union members act for the good of the firm and under the direction of the firm's management team during the agreed-on hours of employment. It also requires that managers and supervisors act in accordance with the terms of the contract. Furthermore, it sets up a joint decider subsystem in the form of a grievance process to resolve disputes about terms of the contract and the way that it is administered.

Creation of a new system. The fourth type of agreed system is a relatively independent living system set up by agreement of two or more other systems. Examples include marriages, partnerships, joint ventures, and supranational systems such as the North Atlantic Treaty Organization

(NATO), the European Union (EU), and the World Court. The goal of negotiations in these cases is to agree on the template of the new system.

Joint venture negotiations are typically very complex, involving questions such as how much authority will be delegated to the agreed system, how much technology transfer will occur, how much and what sort of capital each partner will contribute, how rapidly the joint venture is expected to grow, and under what conditions it might be dissolved. In many cases, the joint venture is given very substantial scope for independent decision making, simply because the partners are unwilling or unable to manage it closely themselves.

THE INTERFACE BETWEEN SYSTEM AND ENVIRONMENT

Thus far we have emphasized beneficial interaction with the environment. Yet many elements in the environment are potentially harmful to an organization. In addition to negotiating advantageous exchanges, managers must protect the organization from threats.

In the context of living systems theory, an organization that lacks strong reactive defenses to environmental threats is equivalent to a person whose "immune system" is not functioning properly. A person lacking immunities may survive for a while with good medical care, but the long-term prognosis is poor. Likewise, a firm with inadequate reactive defenses may limp along with infusions of capital and help from consultants. Yet in order to maintain its health in the long run, an organization must develop structures and processes that provide some degree of immunity from external threats.

Small organizations typically have only generalized reactive defenses. Like an infant whose immunities come primarily from the mother, a newly hatched firm is dependent on its founders for the strength and expertise required for its defense. As an organization grows, however, it typically develops specific processes and structures that provide reactive defenses against various external threats and internal disruptions. We call these defenses the organizational *immunity subsubsystem* (IS).

The IS is a subsystem of an organization's boundary subsystem. The boundary "separates the system from its environment. It surrounds and protects vulnerable components, acts as a barrier to free movement of matter, energy, and information in and out of the system, and filters inputs and outputs by allowing some but not others to pass."[1]

As a separator, the boundary is at the *interface* between the living system and its environment. In its simplest form, the boundary consists of a layer or layers of material between the system's other components and its environment. In organizations, however, it is generally more complex than that. Aside from walls and fences, the boundary of an organization consists of those members whose job is to deal directly with the environment.

Selective Input and Output

The boundary of a living system must be selective about what it lets into and out of the system. Selectivity is very important for the immunity processes of the system. The boundary subsystem is supposed to protect other parts of the system from environmental stresses.

The boundary is especially useful in filtering out excessive amounts of potentially harmful inputs and preventing the loss of needed resources. As an example of the former process, organizations guard against excessive information input by screening letters and phone calls. Inventory controls are used to defend against pilferage.

Reactive protection processes may also extend beyond the surface or occur within the system. A manufacturer receiving subassemblies of inferior quality may seek to alleviate the stress by finding another supplier, rather than by screening shipments and rejecting substandard goods after they have already been received. A firm may decide to institute random in-plant drug testing for all employees rather than, or in addition to, trying to select applicants who are drug free.

When a living system tries to protect itself well beyond or within the perimeter of the system, can these processes still be ascribed to the boundary subsystem? Although Miller and Miller define a system's boundary as being "at its perimeter,"[2] I have suggested elsewhere that it would be better to say the boundary is at the interface between the system and its environment, wherever that interface may occur.[3] An element of the environment that penetrates the outermost layer becomes an *inclusion,* but it does not become a component of the system until it passes the innermost layer.[4] For instance, a sales representative of another firm is allowed to enter the premises of NewVent, but is kept off the production floor and out of the research and development (R&D) labs.

Organizational Immunity Processes

Immunity processes are a function of the boundary subsystem and can be ascribed to the IS. Immunity processes are the last line of defense. When an inclusion gets past or is accepted by the IS, it becomes a component of the system. The IS is a primary center for *adjustment processes,* which "maintain steady states in systems, keeping variables within their ranges of stability despite stresses."[5]

Immunity involves distinguishing between nonsystem inclusions (i.e., foreign material) and components of the system, recognizing whether inclusions are potentially harmful or beneficial, and treating them accord-

Layers of Defense

Skin, hair, and nails are part of the outer layer of defense for human beings. The skin provides few openings to the interior; frequent washing and grooming also reduce threats. Taste, smell, appearance, and texture provide clues to the presence of a harmful substance and cause it not to be ingested. The epiglottis closes to prevent harmful matter from invading the lungs.

Organizations likewise employ outer boundary layers to restrict entry of potentially harmful matter-energy and information. Gates with guards, locked doors and windows, fences with alarm systems, receptionists, computer access codes, and employment application forms and interviews are common forms of first-line passive defense in organizations. This aspect of organizational defense is generally quite adequate. It doesn't stop everything that is potentially harmful from entering the organization, but it is not expected to. Outer defenses sufficiently elaborate to stop every intruder would probably be too expensive and would also prevent too many vital resources from entering.

The second line of defense in organisms is the IS. The outer layer of the IS in many organisms consists of a supply of general-purpose defenders (e.g., complement and macrophages) that circulate in the blood stream. When one of these defenders detects an intruder, others converge on the site of the problem. Their task is to isolate and transform the intruder, if possible, or to hold it off until more specialized defenders can be produced.

A similar function is served in communities by police patrol officers who keep watch for suspicious activities, accidents, traffic violations, and so forth. When a serious offense occurs, they call in other officers to help out. Finally, specialists such as a detective, a forensic team, a bomb squad, or a negotiator may be summoned.

In business organizations, this second line of defense is generally provided by operative employees and their supervisors. If properly trained, these members are capable of detecting potentially harmful situations, sounding the alarm, and beginning the process of containing the problem. For example, a machine operator may be trained to spot a malfunction, stop the machine, report the problem to the supervisor, and even initiate minor repairs. Likewise, a sales clerk may learn how to spot a customer in the act of shoplifting and detain or distract the thief while calling for the assistance of a supervisor or guard.

Part of a supervisor's job may be to watch for external threats, such as union organizers, bad checks, and materials or workmanship that do not meet specifications. The supervisor may also be expected to look for internal disruptions such as machinery malfunction, failure to adhere to budgets and schedules, loafing, and fighting. Finally, the supervisor may be trained to cope with minor incidents and to alert authorities if there is any escalation.

The performance of second-line defenses in organizations depends on good design and proper training. Operative employees are often in the best position to spot problems early, before serious damage is done to the organization or its equipment. Yet many organizations do not include defense duties in the design of operative jobs, and do not train employees to detect problems and take appropriate action on them. Business firms often rely too heavily on supervisors for detection of problems, at the expense of response time. Supervisors may become overloaded, being confronted with too many problems at once.

The first layer of the IS should be able to detect all external threats that reach it. These general defenders should not be expected to cope with every variety of threat that may present itself, however. In many cases the role of the first layer is simply to sound the alarm and try to hold off the threat until specialized forces can be brought into play. Thus, the IS must have, or have access to, a second layer of defense for difficult threats and disruptions.

The immune systems of higher organisms demonstrate good design principles for the second layer of the IS. When a known antigen is detected, antibodies designed specifically to destroy that antigen are quickly cloned. The antibody prototype may have been developed during an earlier infection or through vaccination. The general defense force has only to hold off the attack while these antibodies are being produced. Thus, rather than maintaining a large reserve force of specialists at high cost, these organisms maintain a smaller set of structures capable of rapidly producing more effective defenders when needed.

This is a lesson that most organizations and societies have yet to learn. Applied to a business firm it would mean that, rather than hiring and training each employee only for a specific function, the firm should provide cross-training so that employees can quickly respond to a variety of emergencies. A manufacturing firm might also maintain a small general-purpose machine shop capable of generating a variety of repair parts or producing small batches of product when urgently needed.

Many organizations tie up a substantial portion of their resources in an elaborate cadre of special defenders—attorneys, security specialists, medical personnel, safety officers, auditors, credit analysts, computer security experts, and human resource management specialists, for example. In some cases, maintenance of such full-time defensive specialists within the organization is justified by the volume of work they must do. In other cases, however, they may spend much of their time waiting for a problem to occur. While waiting they tend to create a lot of busy work for themselves and others, or to generate problems in other ways.

Judging from the organismic model, a key to good design of IS defenses is to maintain on full-time status no more specialists than can be kept usefully busy, and be prepared to generate or import more of them when needed. The general defenders must be capable of holding off a threat long enough for special defenders to be located or produced. Instead of maintaining a department of full-time firefighters, for instance, a large manufacturing facility might train regular employees as reserves for this role, instruct all employees in emergency procedures, and maintain only a small cadre of experts to plan and direct the process. Evacuation procedures and insurance would provide a backup line of defense in case all else fails.

Training is the organizational equivalent of vaccination. Good training gives employees a taste of various threats and problems, allowing the employees to detect these dangers more quickly and rehearse responses to them.

Training for immunity comes in many forms. The traditional fire drill is an example, although it focuses more on individual safety than on fighting the fire. Chain stores and franchisers employ inspectors who pose as customers, rate the service they receive, and provide feedback to the servers. There are many methods used to "vaccinate" employees, but there are probably many more as yet untried.

Dispersal of Immunity Processes

Some defense specialties cannot easily be learned and held in reserve. You cannot expect attorneys to learn the law and then hold that knowledge while they perform other tasks in the organization. Yet the organization may not need a full-time patent attorney, for instance.

People cope with this problem by dispersing certain processes to other individuals and organizations. Living systems are not required to possess a full set of critical subsystems and processes. They may survive so long as they possess their own decider subsystem and have access to all other critical processes. Thus, people do not have to learn for themselves such special protective processes as medicine and law, so long as physicians and attorneys are readily available. But they do need to know enough to realize when the specialist is needed.

Organizations must allocate resources wisely. Rather than maintaining a large cadre of defensive specialists, a business firm should in many cases simply ensure access to specialized services provided by other organizations and consultants. A law firm is retained for legal services when needed. A contract is signed with an emergency medical service and a hospital for emergency health care services. Temporary employment firms provide extra clerical help when an excess of data input and output threatens to clog the system.

> *Specialized organizations provide a pool of trained defenders who can be allocated when and where they are needed. To make this strategy work, however, someone in the firm must be expert in determining what specialists are needed and where and how they can be obtained quickly.*

Avoiding Pathologies of Immunity Processes in Organizations

It appears that organization designers and managers should pay more attention to pathologies of the IS. In designing immunity processes and building structures to carry them out, decision makers should consider the need to

1. *accurately detect and recognize potentially harmful stresses and deviations,*
2. *respond with sufficient strength to negate the threat,*
3. *avoid wasting resources,* and
4. *allow for moderate change or for overriding control by the decider so that the system can respond to a dynamic environment.*

To illustrate some of these design problems, consider the typical human resource management department in a business firm. It serves several functions for the IS. For instance, it monitors the labor market, keeping track of competitive wage rates and labor shortages; it attempts to select applicants who will be productive members of the organization, and to reject those who will not; it attempts to correct deviant behavior by administering discipline and providing training; it handles grievances and tries to ensure that employees are treated fairly; and it may conduct periodic surveys of employee attitudes, attempting to detect problems that need to be addressed. Each of these duties involves detecting potential external threats or internal disruptions and attempting to cope with them. Yet in each of these duties the system may malfunction.

Accurately distinguishing between applicants who will become productive employees and those who will not is a chronic problem. Millions of dollars are spent annually on weighted application blanks, tests, interviews, and assessment centers, yet the results are very modest. These selection devices typically account for less than 30 percent of the variance in subsequent performance and are often accused of discriminating on the basis of race or national origin and falsely rejecting good applicants.[6]

Selection procedures also may become calcified and unable to respond to changes in the work force. Thus, the ability to detect potentially harmful inputs and to distinguish them from beneficial ones is weak, at best. Yet most business firms devote considerable resources to recruitment and selection of employees, believing that failure to do so would be even more costly.

We may also question whether the typical human resource department does an adequate job of coping with internal disruptions. The disciplinary system, sometimes in conjunction with counseling and training, is supposed to correct employee behavior when it deviates from the norm, but the system often fails to do so. Sometimes the failure lies in detection; supervisors and others who should be monitoring employee performance simply fail to perceive poor behavior or choose to ignore it. In other cases, the discipline is not effective; it is not accepted as equitable and deserved, or it is considered to be of little consequence.

Organization designers should consider whether it is wise to separate certain human resource functions from the job of supervisor. A well-trained supervisor might be more effective than human resource experts in employee selection, because the supervisor is better attuned to the behavioral dynamics and task requirements of the job that is being filled. Likewise, the supervisor might be better at administering effective discipline, being more aware of how the individual employee is likely to respond to a particular penalty. Indeed, with proper training the work force might also be involved in disciplinary procedures.

There should be a backup system, of course. Experts are needed to train supervisors in these tasks, to monitor the supervisors' performance, and to provide an avenue of appeal when supervisors lose objectivity. The basic point is that the design of human resource management functions should carefully consider what belongs to the outer layer of the IS (i.e., the supervisor and the work group) and what the inner layer of human resource specialists must be prepared to do.

Organizations would also do well to consider more cross-training of members in reserve functions, as well as greater emphasis on culture as a unifying influence. Over-reliance on specialized detection and control mechanisms may result in defenses that are too slow—they detect the damage after it is already done—and too costly. Many effective business firms have put much of the detection and correction processes directly in the hands of operative employees, relying on their skills and their commitment to organizational goals to ensure adequate defense of the organization. In doing so, they have added an extra outer layer to the traditional layers of the IS in organizations.

Practical Suggestions

The structures and processes associated with immunity in living systems are part of the boundary subsystem. Given the abundance of life-threatening environmental stresses and internal strains on all living systems, these protective structures and processes are critical and deserve much attention. Particularly at the level of organizations, where immunity processes and structures are mostly artificial, more consideration should be given to design in order to avoid pathologies and provide sufficient coverage at a reasonable cost.

Specific suggestions for improvement of the IS in organizations include:

1. *Provide several layers of protection. The outer layer should be proactive, attempting to prevent or avoid threats and disruptions. The next layer(s) may be passive, selective, relatively inexpensive, and easy to maintain. Only severe or unusual threats and disruptions should reach and trigger the innermost, reactive layers of the IS.*
2. *The IS should have at least two layers. The outer IS layer should consist of generalists capable of detecting and identifying threats, and holding them at bay while the inner layer generates or imports specialized defenses. The organization should not try to maintain full-scale specialized defenses for a wide variety of threats, unless it is specifically a defense organization.*
3. *All members of the organization can be part of the IS, particularly if they are committed to its goals. The organization should maintain a strong culture and employ training extensively to familiarize employees with various potential dangers, keep them alert, and enable them to rehearse their responses. Such training will shorten the response time and increase the defensive reserves of the organization.*
4. *The organization should have planned access to various protective specialists whose skills are not needed on a full-time basis, such as attorneys, consultants, trainers, physicians, insurance advisors, and safety experts.*
5. *The design of the IS should be concerned both with effectiveness of protection and with avoidance of pathologies. The IS should not make the system too rigid, or attack components of the system, or require excessive resources.*

NOTES

1. James G. Miller and Jessie L. Miller, "Greater than the sum of its parts," *Behavioral Science* 37 (1992): 23.

2. Ibid.

3. Lane Tracy, "Immunity and error correction: System design for organizational defense," *Systems Practice* 6 (1993): 259–74.

4. James G. Miller, *Living Systems* (New York: McGraw-Hill, 1978), 33.

5. Ibid., 35.

6. John E. Hunter and Ronda F. Hunter, "Validity and utility of alternative predictors of job performance," *Psychological Bulletin* 96 (1984): 72–98.

Chapter 9

Managing Problems of Leadership

As the general manager of NewVent, Terry has many people dependent on his decisions. UniGlobe's investors hold him responsible for making a profit and generating income. He also feels responsibility toward his employees, many of whom have been with the firm since its inception. His own income and the livelihood of his wife and children are also dependent on his decisions.

In addition, several auto manufacturers depend on NewVent to deliver high-quality units on time. The firms that supply raw materials rely on NewVent for continued orders. The bank that gives NewVent a line of credit depends on the firm to repay the loans. Terry's decisions affect each of these firms. Finally, Terry feels a loyalty to the community, the nation, and his religious group. Is it possible for Terry, as the leader of the firm, to make decisions that represent all of these diverse interests?

MULTIPLE CONSTITUENCIES

As we noted in Chapter 7, the various individuals, groups, and organizations that hold an interest in a firm's activities are called its stakeholders or constituencies.[1] Figure 9-1 displays some of the many stakeholder pressures that other social systems and individuals exert on the decisions of a typical business firm.

One modern approach to the assessment of organizational effectiveness, the multiple-constituency approach, measures the success of the firm according to how well it serves each of these constituencies.[2]

Figure 9-1
Stakeholder Pressures on a Typical Business Firm

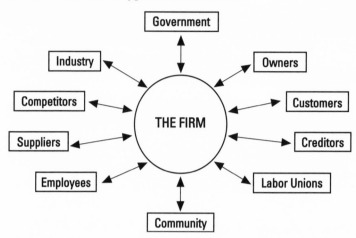

Source: Lane Tracy, "Design for organizational health," *Journal of Business Research* no. 12
     (1992): 62. Used by permission of the Research Institute Administration Office, College
     of Economics, Nihon University, Tokyo, Japan.

Table 9-1 lists criteria that might be used by each constituency to measure
the effectiveness of the firm in satisfying their needs.

Table 9-1
Effectiveness Criteria Used by Various Constituencies of a Firm

Constituency	Effectiveness Criteria
1. Owners	Financial return, growth
2. Employees	Work satisfaction, pay, supervision
3. Customers	Quality of goods and services, price
4. Creditors	Credit rating, assets
5. Community	Contribution to community affairs
6. Suppliers	Regular orders, good price
7. Government	Obedience to laws and regulations, taxes

It is obvious that the firm and its leaders cannot serve all constituencies
equally well. When the interests of various constituencies diverge, leaders must make some hard decisions. A great amount of strain and conflict, both within and between systems, may be generated by these
choices.

Leaders of social systems are the focus of conflicting interests. Consequently, leaders play a primary role in the management of conflict, both within the systems they lead and between systems. Leaders make key decisions that can either resolve conflict or intensify it.

Yet leaders are often in a state of internal conflict with regard to whom they represent. They are expected to make decisions for the benefit of the particular group, organization, community, or society that they lead. But they must also make decisions for their own benefit. In addition, they may be the chief decision makers for a family, a political party, a subgroup of owners or executives, and so forth. I call this the problem of divided loyalty of leaders.

What effect does divided loyalty have on the ability of leaders to manage conflict? How can social systems be structured to manage the conflicts that leaders face within themselves? Let us now examine these questions in detail.

LEADERSHIP AND LIVING SYSTEMS

The decider of any complex living system is hierarchical and has many echelons or levels. The decider subsystems of mammals, for instance, have nine echelons ranging from the cerebral cortex at the top to the endocrine glands and certain neurons at the bottom. Similarly, large organizations have echelons such as a board of directors, chief executive officer, vice presidents, managers, department heads, supervisors, and operative employees. An organization chart is essentially a diagram of an organization's formal decider subsystem. It should be recognized, however, that an informal hierarchy often exists and that many decisions may be made without reference to the formal hierarchy.

Decision making occurs at all echelons of the decider. You are probably most aware of the deciding that is done by your cerebral cortex, but in fact many of your body processes are controlled locally without direction from any part of your brain. Similarly, in any organization members at the lowest echelon, such as sales clerks and machine operators, must make many decisions in order to carry out their work. It would be inefficient to require that every move be approved by a supervisor, just as it would be inefficient to require that every heartbeat be controlled by the brain.

As we move upward in the hierarchy, the decision-making domain becomes broader and decisions have greater consequences. By the same token, however, the upper echelons do not have time to devote to the frequent, detailed decisions required to carry out mundane processes.

In Chapter 2 we noted that the decision-making process encompasses the following four stages:

1. establishing purposes and goals,
2. receiving and analyzing information,
3. synthesizing plans and choosing a course of action, and
4. implementing the choice by transmitting commands.

The first stage, the setting of purposes and goals, is often carried out separately and in advance of the other stages. Nonetheless, it is an essential stage of the decider process, because deviations cannot exist without standards or preferred steady states. A model of the process by which purposes and goals lead to decisions and thence to motivated behavior was presented in Chapter 3.

It should be evident that the four stages of the decider process, taken in the context of a social system, constitute what is generally expected of a leader. That is, a leader sets goals for the system, analyzes alternatives, makes choices, and issues orders to implement those choices. Some writers on leadership emphasize the goal-setting aspect, picturing leaders as visionaries and guiding lights. Other writers focus on the choices that leaders make; good leaders are those who make effective or popular choices for the system. Still others see leadership primarily in terms of implementation; leaders display the skills of persuasion that are necessary to induce other people to work for the system's goals.

In my opinion, leadership includes *all* of the stages of the decider process for a social system. Analysis and choice without clear goals is dangerous. Proceeding directly from goals to action without any intervening analysis is foolhardy. Planning without implementation is useless.

A single leader may not be able to supply all of the stages of the decider process, but the system requires leadership that, collectively, encompasses all of these stages. Thus, I define *leadership* as "purposeful assumption of some or all of the processes of the top echelon of the decider subsystem for a group, organization, [community], society, or supranational system."[3] There are many other definitions of leadership, but this one has the advantages of being rooted in living systems theory and of providing a more complete picture of leadership.

Leadership in organizations generally is supplied by founders, chief executives, executive committees, and boards of directors. Entrepreneurial founders of new businesses, for example, must specify goals for the nascent organization, analyze the market, provide ideas for meeting those goals, and issue orders about (or show by example) what must be done. Boards of directors establish values and set goals, but usually leave the other stages of leadership to the executives. Executives or their staffs gather data and analyze it; then an executive committee may put together a plan that is issued over the signature of the chief executive.

The exact distribution of leadership tasks varies from one firm to another, and even from one instance to another. However the tasks may be shared, organizational leadership is provided by one person or a small group of people at the top of the organization's hierarchy.

This point is hardly surprising. What might be less obvious is the fact that there are many other leaders in the typical organization. Large organizations, at least, contain many groups and suborganizations (e.g., divisions, departments) as components. Each of these groups and suborganizations is, itself, a living system and each has one or more leaders in its own right. These multiple levels of leadership pose problems for the leader(s) of the host organization.

CONFLICT AND LIVING SYSTEMS

Conflict, as we saw in Chapter 7, is a strain arising within a system when it receives two or more incompatible commands. For example, two groups of stockholders may make incompatible demands on the chief executive officer (CEO); three customers may simultaneously demand service from a lone clerk; two departments may each require three fourths of the organization's available research funds; the buyer for a customer may demand a payoff that violates the sales representative's ethical values.

Incompatible commands may come from self, suprasystems (e.g., the government), subsystems, same-level systems, or any combination of these. In the example of the payoff demand, a command from a same-level system (the buyer) is vying with an internal command from the sales representative's conscience. Legal commands from the government and policy commands from the employer may also be involved.

Another point to note is that the strain may be felt by the whole system or any component of it. In the payoff instance, the strain at first affects only the sales representative. If she reports the demand to her supervisor, however, the strain may soon be felt in many parts of the organization.

Generators of Conflict

Because issuing commands or suggestions is one of the stages of leadership, it can be seen that leaders not only experience conflict but also often generate it. Three common characteristics of living-systems leadership that tend to cause conflict are

1. each level of a complex, hierarchical social system has its own leadership;
2. leadership of a social system may be shared by two or more leaders; and
3. leaders are living systems in their own right.[4]

Let us examine each of these conflict-generating characteristics in turn.

Multiple levels. Complex social systems are composed of subsystems and components, such as departments, bureaus, and political subdivisions, that are also living systems. Each department and bureau within an organization has its own leaders.

Such multiple levels of leadership are an obvious source of conflict, because leaders at each level are making decisions and issuing commands based, in part, on the goals and purposes of their own system. The goals and purposes of the subdivisions may be aligned with those of the organization, but the alignment is never perfect. Thus, a sales manager may issue a command to traveling sales representatives to increase the number of calls they make, thereby increasing sales and commissions, while at the same time the CEO commands the representatives to spend more time with each client in order to improve service. Both leaders are attempting to serve what they perceive as the needs of the organization, but they have different perspectives on those needs.

Leaders not only generate conflicting commands from different levels of the organization, but also receive them. For instance, a production supervisor may receive orders from the comptroller to economize and from the vice president of marketing to hold more finished units in inventory. Or the supervisor may receive orders from above for increased production while hearing demands from employees for a decrease in overtime. The different perspectives of suprasystems and subsystems are a source of myriad strains.

Shared leadership. The definition of leadership asserts that a leader assumes *some or all* of the processes of decision making. These processes may be divided and shared in a number of ways. The board of directors may set goals, staff members may analyze data, and the CEO may then make a choice and issue orders. Leadership may fall to a group (e.g., an executive committee) or be exercised equally by partners in a business. Although the individuals and groups who share leadership may cooperate with one another, the fact that they are separate living systems with their own purposes and goals means that some conflict among leaders is inevitable.

Shared leadership engenders conflict when the leaders issue incompatible commands to each other or to subsystems and components. When the president of the United States demands new taxes to balance the budget but Congress favors cuts in services instead, a great deal of strain is provoked in the nation. Similarly, strain is induced in employees when two partners who are the joint owners of the firm give the employees incompatible tasks to do.

Divided loyalty. The fact that leaders are living systems means that every social system must share its leader (and other echelons of its decider subsystem) with at least one other system. Leaders must make decisions for themselves as well as for the social systems that they lead. In some cases a person is leader of two or more social systems as well. The prime minister of Japan, for example, is also the leader of his political party.

This sharing of the leader or decider function by two or more living systems causes two different sorts of problems. First, the attention of the leader may be elsewhere when the social system requires it. Second, the loyalty of the leader may be divided by incompatible demands of the two or more systems that she serves.

The loss of the leader's attention generates conflict or strain within the system. For example, if the CEO is not present to make a critical decision, because he is asleep or serving another system, there may be a power struggle among those in the next echelon to determine who will make the decision in the CEO's absence, or the system may suffer continued strain while the decision is delayed.

Divided loyalty creates conflict within leaders. Assuming that they don't simply abandon leadership of the social system and act for personal gain, leaders must somehow reconcile the conflicting demands of self and social system(s). This is somewhat similar to role/value conflict, which we discussed in Chapter 7, but divided loyalty is deeper. Leaders are at least partially responsible for defining the leader's role as well as the organizational values and goals on which a decision for the organization should be based. Thus, the role demands come from within just as the personal values do.

Change and Conflict

In addition to the strains generated by multiple levels of leadership, shared leadership, and divided loyalty, leaders are in the business of creating strain within organizations in order to produce change. Whether in response to changes in the environment or in order to move an organization toward realizing its own potential, leaders often define new goals and choose plans of action that will cause large strains in the system. Indeed, leaders who do not periodically generate change are often regarded as mere caretakers or figureheads, not true leaders at all.

A leader may consider strain and conflict to be a necessary part of the change process, but other members of the social system may view such strain and conflict as a problem. In fact, the leader may be depending on members to see it that way so that they will be motivated to make changes.

An unfortunate side effect of the process is that the leader is often regarded as part of the problem and is drawn into the conflict. That is, the leader is seen as giving commands that are incompatible with the dictates of the existing system. One way to resolve such conflict is, of course, to get rid of the leader. Therefore, when deliberately generating conflict, *leaders must be careful to manage it so that changing the current system is always seen as a better option than changing the leader.*

MANAGING LEADERSHIP CONFLICTS

Several methods are commonly used to manage the many inevitable leadership conflicts that occur in organizations. These strategies include compartmentalization of responsibilities, prioritization, homogenization of values and interests, and establishment of checks and balances. Let us examine each strategy in turn.

Compartmentalization

One method commonly employed to try to avoid or manage shared-leadership and multiple-level conflicts is

Define clearly the domain of decision making for each position of leadership and limit each leader's authority to the prescribed domain.

For example, the legislative branch of government establishes the laws and the executive branch implements them. One business partner handles the finances while another deals with personnel and operations. One manager controls the day shift and another the night shift. The supervisor makes daily work assignments, but the department manager is in charge of long-range production scheduling.

Such compartmentalization of responsibilities greatly reduces the potential for conflict, but does not eliminate it. The activities of any living system must still be closely integrated. Thus:

The decisions of multiple leaders, however they may be compartmentalized, must be closely coordinated.

In a hierarchically organized system, the top echelon typically provides coordination, backed by power and authority. Coordination may be attained in cases of shared leadership by devices such as frequent communication, meetings, consensual group decision making, and mediation. Elevating one of the leaders to a position of greater authority is another possible solution.

Compartmentalization is also employed to manage conflicts generated by divided loyalty and opposing interests. Leaders often try to avoid taking their work home with them. While at the office, they make decisions for the sake of the organization; while at home or on lunch break, they make decisions for themselves or the family. Likewise, they make organizational decisions based on organizational values and personal decisions based on personal values.

The success of this strategy depends on how well leaders are able to compartmentalize their lives and employ different values at different times. Leaders are often criticized for abandoning their personal values when they act for the organization, yet living systems theory suggests that such compartmentalization is sometimes necessary.

Temporal compartmentalization, such as the CEO making decisions for the organization only from 9 A.M. to 5 P.M., may create a problem for the organization. During the rest of the day and night the organization as a whole is without leadership. There may be lower-echelon deciders on duty at other hours, such as assistant managers or guards, but the scope of their decision making is limited. In emergencies requiring broad authority, it would probably be necessary to call on the CEO, just as an individual roused from sleep by the smell of smoke would have to assume conscious control.

In general, organizations should make provisions for situations in which the CEO and other leaders are unavailable, whether because they are asleep, incapacitated, out of town, or engaged by other concerns. One method is to

Designate a deputy leader to make decisions in the leader's absence.

In an emergency, when other leaders are unavailable or unable to perform their duties, the deputy leader should have all the authority the other leaders would have. An example is the legal provision whereby the vice-president of the United States can temporarily take over executive duties when the president is incapacitated. Such a provision helps to prevent the conflict that might occur if two or more persons or groups attempt to fill the leadership vacuum created by an absent or incapacitated leader.

Prioritization

Compartmentalization becomes increasingly difficult as the demands of one system become more insistent. The owner of a business or the president of a nation may find that "his time is not his own." When a leader's health or marriage is threatened by overwork, she may find it difficult to maintain the separation of domains.

Writers on leadership have noted that great leaders often emerge in times of crisis. My explanation of this phenomenon is that a crisis in a nation or an organization causes its leaders to focus their attention on the needs of the social system, temporarily subordinating their own needs. That is, a new set of priorities is invoked.

In ordinary times, compartmentalization can work, but it requires a certain amount of good management. That is:

Leaders must establish priorities in order to manage the conflicting demands of social systems and self.

When the demands of all systems cannot be met, the leader must choose which master to serve first.

Many leaders will give priority to their own interests, if such a choice must be made. That is, temporary or permanent abandonment of the leadership role is a primary mode of conflict management for leaders. A leader who subordinates her own interests to the good of the organization is deemed a hero, because such behavior is uncommon.[5]

Given that heroes are rare, social systems have a problem. How can they protect themselves from abandonment by their leaders in times of conflict?

Homogenization of Values and Interests

Leaders often try to manage this problem by means of their role in setting values, purposes, and goals for the organization. That is:

Leaders may try to establish organizational values that are consonant with personal and family values.

A business owner, for example, may try to establish an organizational culture based on personal values.[6] A political leader may use the media to impart personal values to the populace. To the extent that leaders are able to attain personal goals through decisions based on social system values, abandonment of leadership becomes unnecessary.

Social systems also try to choose or grow leaders who embody the values of the group, organization, community, or society. Research on the link between group leaders and conformity to group norms has found that leaders are high in conformity, both because leaders tend to influence the norms and because groups tend to choose leaders who embody the existing norms.[7] Japanese systems of management, emphasizing lifelong employment and slow promotions, may be seen as elaborate methods for growing top managers who are infused with the spirit and values of the company.[8] In a democratic society, the voters tend to elect leaders who espouse values similar to their own.

Choosing leaders whose values match those of the members and providing a long period of socialization for future leaders are prime methods of ensuring harmony between leaders' values and those of the organization.

A related method of resolving the conflict in favor of the social system so that its leaders will not abandon it is

Make the rewards of leadership so attractive that the leaders' interests become fused with those of the organization.

For instance, corporations attempt to structure the rewards of the CEO and other corporate leaders so that decisions benefiting the corporation also benefit its leaders.

This method of conflict management may backfire, if not handled carefully. It breaks down the compartmentalization between personal decisions and decisions for the social system. The leader may begin to think that *all* corporate values are consonant with personal values. Decisions then are based on the belief that "what is good for me is good for the company." Because the individual and the corporation are separate and distinct living systems, however, this belief cannot be entirely true. There may be substantial convergence of interests, but there must also be divergent interests.

Eliminating conflicts caused by the divided loyalty of leaders does not seem to be the best method of conflict management. As with other forms of conflict, there may be benefits both to the organization and to its leader(s) in maintaining certain conflicting interests and values. Organizations often gain from infusion of different values from new leaders, particularly if the environment is changing.[9]

Dictatorships and owner-managed business firms may deteriorate or become involved in harmful conflict with other systems precisely because the leader is unable to distinguish between personal interests and those of the social system. For instance, a business owner who is nearing retirement may lose interest in maintaining the vitality of the business or providing for management succession.

Checks and Balances

To avoid problems such as these, successful social systems tend to develop checks and balances that moderate the power of leaders and subsystems. Pluralism of interests and values is encouraged. No leader is given absolute control, nor are leaders encouraged to identify themselves completely with the social system. Instead, leadership processes are divided and shared, as in the division of responsibilities between a corporate CEO and the board of directors, or the constitutional division of powers among the executive, legislative, and judicial branches of the U. S. government.

Under a system of checks and balances, leaders are required to consult with each other, to negotiate, and to obtain consent before acting on behalf of the social system. Control processes operate to monitor leaders' decisions and their consequences. A set of corporate policies or laws is promulgated to offer formal guidelines for decision making and to provide a basis for adjudication, if necessary. Dynamic tension among conflicting interests is maintained and becomes a source of strength in the living social system.

Specifically with respect to the problem of divided loyalty of leaders:

> *Conflict management strategy should be based on recognition of the fact that it is neither possible nor desirable to eliminate divided loyalty as a source of conflict.*

Leaders *must* represent both themselves and the social systems they lead. Their interests cannot fully coincide with those of the organization.

A certain amount of strain generated by differing values, purposes, and goals is healthy both for social systems and for their leaders. Social systems should not expect absolute loyalty from leaders or any other part of the decider subsystem, but should provide a set of checks and balances whereby conflicts can be discussed, negotiated, adjudicated, and controlled. If this set of checks and balances works properly, the strain on leaders should not become excessive.

LEADERSHIP OF CHANGE

Checks and balances are good for the organization under normal circumstances, but they may get in the way when the situation calls for creative leadership. If the organization is in need of renewal, for instance, shared leadership and other restraints may hamper the efforts of a leader to make the necessary changes. How can the organization recognize when fundamental change is needed? How can the checks and balances be overridden in times of crisis?

To some extent crisis generates awareness of a need for change. When an organization is in severe decline, that is generally apparent to everyone. Members are likely to be looking for someone to lead them out of the crisis. A leader who can put together a plausible plan of action to reverse the tide may find little opposition and substantial motivation for change.

A more difficult situation faces a leader who sees a need for change in a successful organization. The response is likely to be "if it isn't broke, don't fix it." Members may be comfortable with the situation as it is and be unmotivated to change. Yet there are many reasons for fixing something that is still working, ranging from routine maintenance to a philosophy of continuous improvement.

To overcome resistance to change, what may be needed is *transformational leadership*.[10] That is, the leader must appeal to the higher interests of the membership and inspire in them a new vision of what the organization can be. This form of leadership emphasizes the stage of formation of new goals and purposes. Without inspiration, the members will remain frozen in their current patterns of behavior.

Along with a new vision, transformational leaders often do things to shake up the system. Using their existing authority they may reorganize the firm or deliberately generate conflict. Such conflict is healthy for the organization, so long as the leader is correct in diagnosing a need for change. Its purpose is to create a sense of crisis and readiness for creative change.

Once the situation is unfrozen, the leader's problem is to steer the changes in a healthy direction and avoid undesirable side effects. As noted earlier, one of the side effects leaders try to avoid is the perception that they are the source of the problem, the solution being to get rid of them.

A recommended method of managing this sort of conflict is

Bring the members of the organization into the change process. Inform them of the need for change and include them in the decision-making process.

There is nothing revolutionary in this advice, but it is often overlooked.

Leaders sometimes assume that, in order to generate needed change, they must engage in Machiavellian manipulations of the organization's members. Yet it has been demonstrated repeatedly that, in many circumstances, allowing people to participate in the change process is more effective. The various components and subsystems emerge from the participative process with a better understanding of what the organization needs and with greater motivation to do whatever is necessary. Indeed, the planned actions may also be more effective because they are based on better information than the leader originally possessed.[11] So long as the actions are in line with the broader vision, the leader should feel satisfied.

When several echelons are allowed to participate in the decision-making process on major decisions for an organization, the leader's role changes. Instead of being the primary analyzer and synthesizer, the leader becomes the manager of the decision process. The manager may still set the purposes and goals on which decisions are made, but analysis, synthesis, and implementation are delegated to the group or organization as a whole. The leader's role is to guide the process, facilitate it, and perhaps specify decision rules and criteria.

For some leaders, the role requirements of participative decision making conflict with their own conception of leadership. From a living systems point of view, however, leadership includes shouldering *any* of the stages of the decider process. Shared leadership is still leadership; in fact it is a very common form of leadership.

SUMMARY

Examining the topics of conflict management, decision making, and leadership from the viewpoint of living systems theory, we find that conflict is inherent and unavoidable in living social systems because of certain characteristics of their decider subsystem. The decider is composed of several echelons corresponding to levels in the hierarchy of the social system. At each echelon choices are made by people or groups for the benefit of the social system. However, these people or groups are living systems in their own right and must also make decisions for themselves. Additionally, they may be leaders of subsystems and may be required to make decisions based on subsystem values, purposes, and goals. Finally, decider processes at any echelon may be divided and shared among two or more leaders.

Conflict is generated in leaders because (1) they must represent the sometimes incompatible interests of two or more living systems, (2) they must often share leadership, and (3) they receive incompatible commands from two or more levels of the hierarchy. Table 9-2 summarizes the range of strategies used by leaders and social systems to manage leader conflict.

Leaders' conflicts are often managed by compartmentalization. Leaders represent different systems at different times and places, decision processes are divided and assigned, and decision-making responsibilities are defined for each echelon. Compartmentalization is often aided by the setting of priorities. Another general conflict-management strategy is to attempt to make the various interests consonant. It appears, however, that the most successful strategy is to encourage a moderate amount of pluralism in the values of the various systems and subsystems, coupled with a set of checks and balances to ensure that all interests are adequately represented.

Conflict management may mean deliberately increasing conflict as well as decreasing it. Conflicting needs and values are sources of mutual benefit through exchange, as we saw in Chapter 7. Leaders also deliberately generate conflict in order to induce needed change in the social system. For leadership of such systemic change it is often effective to involve several echelons of the decider subsystem in the planning process.

Table 9-2
Organizational Strategies for Managing Leader Conflict

Strategy	Description
Role specification	Define clearly the domains of decision making for each position of leadership.
Coordination	Coordinate multiple leaders by devices such as frequent communication, meetings, consensual group decision making, and mediation, or by elevating one of the leaders to a position of greater authority.
Compartmentalization	Separate organizational decisions from personal decisions. Make organizational decisions based on organizational values and personal decisions on personal values.
Prioritization	Establish clear priorities in order to manage the conflicting demands of social systems and self.
Homogenization of values	Establish organizational or societal values that are consonant with personal and family values.
Personification	Choose or grow leaders who embody the values of the group, organization, community, or society.
Cooptation	Make the rewards of leadership so attractive that the leaders' interests become fused with those of the organization.
Checks and balances	Develop checks and balances that moderate the power of leaders and subsystems.

NOTES

1. Ian I. Mitroff, *Stakeholders of the Organizational Mind* (San Francisco: Jossey-Bass, 1983).

2. Terry Connolly, Edward J. Conlon, and Stuart J. Deutsch, "Organizational effectiveness: A multiple-constituency approach," *Academy of Management Review* 5 (1980): 211–17.

3. Lane Tracy, *The Living Organization: Systems of Behavior* (New York: Praeger, 1989), 141.

4. Ibid., 142–49.

5. Eugene E. Jennings, *An Anatomy of Leadership: Princes, Heroes, and Supermen* (New York: McGraw-Hill, 1960), 70–91.

6. Edgar H. Schein, *Organizational Culture and Leadership: A Dynamic View* (San Francisco: Jossey-Bass, 1991), 209–22.

7. Bernard M. Bass, *Bass and Stogdill's Handbook of Leadership: Theory, Research, and Managerial Applications,* 3d ed. (New York: Free Press, 1990), 606–7.

8. William G. Ouchi and Alfred M. Jaeger, "Type Z organizations: Stability in the midst of mobility," *Academy of Management Review* 3 (1978): 305–14.

9. Gerald R. Salancik, Barry M. Staw, and Louis R. Pondy, "Administrative turn-over as a response to unmanaged organizational interdependence," *Academy of Management Journal* 23 (1980): 422–37.

10. James M. Burns, *Leadership* (New York: Harper & Row, 1978); Noel Tichy and M. Devanna, *Transformational Leadership* (New York: Wiley, 1986).

11. Victor H. Vroom and Arthur G. Jago, *The New Leadership: Managing Participation in Organizations* (Englewood Cliffs, NJ: Prentice-Hall, 1988).

Chapter 10

Managing Change

NewVent has undergone many changes in the four years since it was founded as a subsidiary of UniGlobe. It has grown rapidly in size and complexity. Much of this change was expected, and provisions for it were included in the original business plan. Yet additional adjustments had to be made because of unexpected events.

One unanticipated event was the discovery by the research and development (R&D) department of a major new use for the magnetic flange principle. This additional application required some unplanned reorganization and expansion to tackle the fresh market potential. Also, a major international competitor entered the original market more quickly than expected; apparently they had been working in secret on a similar technological breakthrough. Competition aroused a greater need to concentrate on marketing and pricing issues, as well as to protect NewVent's patents.

Managers and other employees at NewVent have accepted most of this change cheerfully. They knew that they were getting into a young and rapidly growing organization when they took the job, and some turbulence was anticipated. Of course, there have been specific instances in which someone balked at a request to change direction or procedures. Coordination between departments has suffered during transition periods and some friction has resulted. By and large, however, Terry is pleased with the way the organization has responded to the challenges it faced.

UniGlobe has been somewhat less happy about the situation, however. Targets and deadlines have been missed, new requests for capital outlays have been forwarded by NewVent, and the future stream of profits has become less predictable, although it may eventually be greater than originally estimated. UniGlobe is hoping that Terry can stabilize both NewVent's own processes and its environment so that there will be fewer surprises in the future.

INEVITABILITY OF CHANGE

One of the defining characteristics of living systems is that "they maintain a steady state of negentropy even though entropic changes occur in them as they do everywhere else."[1] Thus they are both static, in the sense that they preserve certain essential aspects of themselves, and dynamic. Dynamism manifests itself both in reaction to entropic processes and in proactive innovation. Maintenance of steady states in an unsteady world requires change.

Usefulness

Physicists are interested in *entropy* within the universe, but a manager's universe is the organization and its immediate environment. What a manager regards as production would be called entropy by a physicist. There is no denying that production is entropic; it consumes available energy. But it also adds value to the product or service by changing the materials or ideas into a more useful configuration.

Usefulness is in the eyes of living systems, not the universe. To a manager, usefulness means, perhaps, that the product can be sold for more money than it cost to produce and sell it. In the manager's universe this is not entropy. A manager's entropy is wasted materials, leaking containers, unsold products, uncollectible bills, inefficient use of time and effort, loss of employee skills through retirement and resignation, obsolescence of machinery and processes, monetary inflation, and outdating of information. In short, a manager's entropy is loss of usefulness of an asset. Maintenance of a steady state of *negentropy*, to a manager, means maintenance of useful assets.

In order to maintain usefulness of its assets, an organization must constantly monitor internal and external processes. Internally the organization is consuming and expelling matter and energy, which must be replaced. A flow of materials and energy into and through the system must be maintained. Furthermore, machines are wearing out or becoming obsolete, energy is being consumed, employees are retiring or quitting, and information is becoming outdated. All of these losses must be countered by action to acquire new materials, machinery, energy, employees, and data, or to preserve and refurbish the current assets.

Action may also be needed to protect assets from external attack or to preserve the value of those assets in the marketplace. Theft of goods; damage by wind, water, and fire; liability lawsuits; and challenges to patents are just a few of the environmental threats that must be countered. Obtaining insurance, lobbying for protective legislation, and establishing new markets are some of the ways in which a firm seeks to control its environment and guard its assets.

Maintaining usefulness may be a reactive or a proactive process. That is, the system can wait until losses occur and then try to counteract them, or it can try to anticipate losses and minimize or redirect them.

Reactive Response to Entropy

Losses are inevitable, but they can be managed to some extent. You cannot stop entropy, but you can replace the assets that have been lost. The key to being able to do this is that replacements are obtainable at less cost than the effort required to obtain them. This condition exists when the replacements are plentiful and essentially free, as when wild animals live off the land. It also exists when the system is profitable; that is, the worth of its outputs in the marketplace is greater than the cost of its inputs.

Most of the resources required by organizations are not free. In order to be able to replace assets lost through entropy, therefore, managers must ensure that the firm is profitable or, in the case of a nonprofit organization, that it attracts donations to offset its losses. This means that the organization, through production and other processes, must add worth to its resources in the eyes of other systems. These other systems must be willing to "buy" the products and services of the organization for more than they cost to produce.

Summing up, two basic principles of *reactive* managed change are that

1. *Assets lost through entropy must be replaced.*
2. *An organization must add worth to its resources sufficient to offset entropic losses.*

Control of Processes

Effective maintenance of living systems ultimately depends on control of critical processes. Entropy applies to processes as well as to matter-energy; that is, processes deteriorate over time if left untended. Waste of materials, energy, and human effort is the result of processes that are out of control.

Controlling processes requires detection of the problem, which may be accomplished either by monitoring a process or by measuring its output and comparing the observations with a standard. Monitoring, measurement, and establishment of standards imply a certain amount of planning and proactivity, but the change process may focus simply on returning the process to its original specifications.

Control is a well-known concept to accountants and production managers. Often, however, managers do not realize that control must be exercised over other organizational processes, such as the information system, the human resource management system, and marketing. Control of processes through feedback is a basic characteristic of living systems. Thus, another principle of reactive managed change is that

3. *Control must be exercised over all critical processes, and process errors must be corrected.*

The sorts of change engendered by the need to counteract entropy may not seem like change at all, because they are directed at maintaining some aspect of the status quo. But in an entropic world, the status quo does not maintain itself. Change occurs willy-nilly, and managed change is necessary to keep the system in alignment.

Reaction to Environmental Change

Thus far we have considered only responses to internal change, but living systems must also react to changes in the environment. Maintaining a constant internal temperature when the external temperature is dropping rapidly, for instance, requires changes in the system to counteract the shift in the environment. One change might be the addition of insulation in order to protect critical internal processes. Yet even insulation will not entirely stop the loss of internal heat; another necessary change may be to increase the internal generation of heat.

To sustain a steady flow of production, a business firm must react to changes in competitive pricing, altered availability of raw materials, development of labor unrest, threats of new competition or a hostile takeover, modifications in orders, shifts in consumer preferences, and upheavals in the economy. Each of these external changes may require a variety of internal adjustments. Accordingly, the fourth principle of reactive managed change is that

4. *An organization must react to environmental changes in such a way as to maintain equilibrium in the organization.*

The four principles of managed change that we have discussed so far are all mandated by the system's maintenance imperative. That is, these change processes are governed by purposes and goals that are based on a living system's drive to preserve its essential nature, despite internal and external changes that are uncontrolled or uncontrollable. In addition to these reactive methods of maintaining the status quo, however, there are also proactive methods.

PROACTIVE MANAGEMENT OF CHANGE

In some cases, it is easier or more effective to influence the environment than to adjust to it. For instance, many organisms build or dig shelter for themselves, rather than trying to respond internally to changes in the weather. Human beings go beyond that by clothing themselves and heating their homes. Thus, management of change is often proactively directed at the environment.

A business firm seeks a large share of the market for its goods and services in part because this gives the firm some control over competition. The firm can defeat or frighten away competitors by underpricing them, offering dealer incentives that they can't match, or overwhelming them with advertising. What the firm is doing is to stabilize its environment.

Other examples of change directed at the environment include lobbying for favorable legislation, entering new markets for purposes of diversification, encouraging competition among vendors, working closely with a single supplier to improve its processes, engaging in a public relations campaign, and aiding local job training programs. These acts illustrate the first principle of *proactive* managed change:

1. *An organization must seek to influence or control its environment for greater stability.*

Instead of reacting to entropy, a living system may seek to direct it. By applying energy and materials—that is, by using up some resources—the system can retard entropic processes elsewhere. For instance, manufacturing firms delay the deterioration of critical machinery by performing routine maintenance. Likewise, the rate of loss and decay in vital raw materials is slowed by proper storage and temperature control. Employees who possess hard-to-replace skills are retained by paying them bonuses, and their skills are up-dated through periodic training. If managers are considered to be integral parts of the organization, whereas hourly paid employees are not, the firm pushes the latter employees to their limit and gets rid of them when they are used up. Thus, the second principle of proactive managed change is

2. *Entropic losses should be shifted from critical assets to less critical assets.*

Assets that are not critical are consumed, ejected as products, or allowed to decay in a normal fashion. The focus of managed change with respect to these assets is to replace them. Inventory is monitored and new goods are ordered as losses occur, or even in anticipation of losses. Machinery is replaced on schedule or in response to a breakdown. Manpower losses are recorded or projected and new employees are hired. This strategy works well so long as the necessary resources are more plentiful outside the system than within it. Thus, the third principle of proactive managed change is

   3. *Entropic losses should be shifted from the system to its environment, if possible.*

Principles 2 and 3 are often applied together. That is, the system acquires resources from its environment to use as *substitutes* for critical assets. Organizations exhibit this combination in a variety of ways. For instance, business firms consume large quantities of energy and raw materials in order to maintain a congenial and productive environment (e.g., air conditioning and comfortable furniture) for their critical human resources. Consumables such as lubricants and human labor are acquired and employed to preserve essential machinery. Unprofitable divisions are sold off in order to obtain capital for the core of the business.

The importance of the second and third principles of proactive management of change can hardly be overemphasized. Living systems live or die by their ability to counteract entropy within themselves. From a universal viewpoint, however, they use up more than their share of resources. That is, they shift their losses to their environment by finding and ingesting large quantities of food, water, oxygen, fuel, raw materials, labor, and other natural resources. Some of these resources, such as food and labor, are themselves the products of living systems doing the same thing. Thus, a "food chain" develops; the higher you rise in the chain, the more your entropic losses are shifted to assets that are plentiful or, at least, belong to someone else.

CHANGE FOR ACTUALIZATION

Thus far we have considered only changes required for maintenance of the system. Yet living systems are born with a template that mandates actualization of the system's potential, as well. An infant cannot remain an infant; it must grow and develop into an adult. Although theoretically a business firm may remain small, if the idea on which it is built is a good one, other systems will practically force the firm to grow or else will replace it with a more adaptable system.

The changes necessary for human physical maturation are directed by our genetic program. Social maturation is guided by the templates of family and community. At the same time, of course, these templates also require the maintenance of many ongoing physical and social processes, such as metabolism and obedience to parents. Obviously, the demands for stability and growth may clash and may be a source of considerable tension in the system. We see this most dramatically, perhaps, in the behavior of adolescents who act like adults one moment and like children the next.

A business firm is expected to expand and become more complex in response to competition and increasing demand for its products and services. Yet it must also strive to maintain current cash flow and efficiency, as well as retain some semblance of order and predictability. The question for managers becomes not only how to maintain the status quo but also how to respond to opportunity. When faced with these conflicting demands, managers may experience the same sort of tension as an adolescent, yet they don't have the luxury of being allowed to act like one.

Programmed Growth

Certain kinds of proactive change are programmed into the system from the beginning. This is obvious in the case of organisms, but it is generally true of organizations as well. Founders of business firms usually anticipate growth of the business and make provisions for it. A new firm may start with excess capacity in its facilities and with an expandable line of credit. A corporation may hold unissued stock in reserve and its charter may provide for eventual expansion of the board of directors. A new unit of an existing corporation, such as NewVent, may be located deliberately in an area where the labor supply is plentiful or distribution facilities are readily accessible, in anticipation of rapid expansion of the market.

Even though organizational expansion is preprogrammed to some extent, it typically requires additional management of the details. Thus, another kind of proactive managed change is programmed growth of the system. The fourth principle of proactive managed change is

4. *In order for the system to grow, components and resources must be added in excess of system losses.*

For instance, employees are hired to fill new positions in addition to replacing employees who leave. Additional machinery is acquired, buildings are expanded or added, new customers are sought, and additional computer terminals are installed and memory is increased.

Programmed Elaboration

Often programmed growth is accompanied by elaboration of the system. The human brain does not simply grow larger, it also becomes more complex and develops new capabilities. The body not only grows but also develops sexual functions. In a business firm, it may be preplanned that, when sales volume of a new product line reaches a certain level, a new division will be formed.

At a minimum, a living system must be at least as complex as the environment with which it is trying to cope. This level of complexity is dictated by Ashby's law of requisite variety. A brief statement of the law is that a regulating system must have at least as much variety as the system that it is trying to regulate.[2]

Growth of a system tends to make both the system and its environment more complex. For instance, addition of employees to an organization means, at a minimum, that more components must be managed; usually it also results in differentiation of functions. The template and/or decider subsystem must become more complex in order to regulate and direct the activities of the expanded system.

A larger organization also tends to come into contact with wider variety in its environment; that is, a larger and more varied assortment of customers, vendors, and competitors. The law of requisite variety indicates that, as an organization grows in size, it must also become more elaborate.

Elaboration occurs not only in the structure of the system, but also in its processes. For instance, total quality management (TQM) is a programmed method for improving system processes (see Chapter 6).[3] Rather than allowing waste to occur and then replacing the loss, or controlling processes and returning them to their original specifications when they vary, TQM attempts to improve processes continuously so that the usefulness of their product is increased. The process improvements are not programmed, but the goal and the method of attaining improvement are preplanned. The TQM process is directed toward continuous elaboration of system processes.

Ideally, the organization is programmed to become more complex as it grows in size. Nevertheless, programmed elaboration usually requires managerial attention. This brings us to the fifth and sixth principles of proactive managed change:

5. *The complexity of the system must be increased in accordance with the increasing variety of its environment.*
6. *The complexity of the template and/or decider subsystem must be increased in accordance with the increasing complexity of the system.*

Management of programmed growth and elaboration is relatively easy, even though it involves deliberate change in the system. The system's template supplies the motive and at least an outline of what must be done. It also legitimizes the efforts of managers to implement the required change.

Unprogrammed Growth

Much more common in organizations, and more difficult to manage, is unprogrammed or spontaneous growth and elaboration. This occurs in situations where either growth was unexpected or else no prior thought was given to the question of how to manage it. Such growth may still be in accordance with the general actualization imperative. The difference is that the decider subsystem must supply all of the directions.

The need for unprogrammed growth may occur through serendipity. Someone in the organization invents a better mousetrap, a key competitor makes a strategic error, or the economy improves and suddenly you have more business than you know what to do with. Or pressure for growth may arise through hard work, which simply pays off more handsomely or more quickly than expected. The need may also sneak up on the organization. You may gradually schedule more and more overtime, or sub-contract more work, until you suddenly realize that there is enough volume to justify another shift or an additional plant.

Organizational growth may also occur through the motivation of managers to increase the scope of their position. Parkinson documented the tendency of organizations to grow even when their product is decreasing.[4] He attributed this phenomenon to the desire of managers to increase the number of their subordinates. Obviously, this sort of unplanned growth needs to be curtailed if the organization is to maintain any semblance of efficiency.

Unprogrammed growth of a firm requires that managers make decisions. First they must recognize the need for expansion. Then they must set a goal—how large should the system be after change has occurred? Next they must choose a set of acts that will reach the goal, presumably by going through the usual processes of information gathering, analysis, and synthesis. Finally, managers must implement the planned set of acts. Often this requires convincing other members of the firm that growth is needed. Altogether, these steps should remind you of our previous discussion of leadership in Chapter 9. In the current context, they constitute the management of unprogrammed growth of the system.

Unprogrammed Elaboration

In the long run, growth requires elaboration of the system. As a firm expands into new markets, for instance, its production lines may become overburdened or its distribution system may be overextended. Managers may perceive a previously unanticipated need to create separate product departments or geographical divisions. This may also entail creation of another layer of management. Such elaboration of the system is usually unprogrammed.

A firm may also be forced into greater complexity by changes in its environment. Increasing government regulation may require establishment of one or more specialized departments to cope with the regulators. Changing technology may cause the firm to set up an R&D department. These elaborations of the system are more than simple adjustments to maintain equilibrium, because they change the structure of the system itself.

Processes may also be the focus of ad hoc elaboration. As technology advances, new and better materials may be introduced that require adaptation, or even complete revamping, of the firm's production processes. Improved machinery or changes in the availability and cost of skilled labor may also require such changes.

Manager-directed changes in structure and process constitute unprogrammed elaboration of the system. It is similar to unprogrammed growth, except that the focus is on modifications that make the organization or its processes more complex. Thus, a seventh principle of proactive managed change is that

> 7. *Managers must recognize the need for unprogrammed growth and elaboration of the system and must be prepared to coordinate it.*

To summarize this section, actualization of a system's potential requires both programmed and unprogrammed change within the system. The change may consist of growth, elaboration, or both.

PROPAGATION

Living systems also act to alter their environment in order to create new opportunities. For instance, nations build roads and waterways in order to provide an infrastructure for economic growth. Business firms create advertising campaigns to prepare consumers for a new product.

Such change processes are in accordance with the propagation imperative. The essence of propagation is *extension of aspects of the system into its environment.*

Reproduction

For organisms, propagation is largely a matter of reproduction. Most organisms are programmed to mate or cross-pollinate in some fashion, thereby fertilizing an egg or seed that will grow into an organism of the same species. Organizations carry out a similar process when they set up joint ventures. A joint venture takes some of its characteristics from each of its parents. If it is successful, it may become an independent entity.

Cells reproduce by cloning. So do many organizations. Franchising is essentially a cloning process whereby copies of the original business are spread across the land. Fraternities and sororities "colonize" by setting up chapters on new campuses. Multinational corporations establish subsidiaries in foreign countries. In each case, the new organization is given a charter or template that is very similar to that of the parent.

Like plants that can reproduce from planting a root or branch, organizations may reproduce by growing a new organization from parts of themselves. For instance, NewVent was put together from bits and pieces of UniGlobe; eventually it may be spun off to create a new corporation.

Organizations also display means of reproduction that are not found at the biological system levels. For example, business firms may create a new firm by merging. The old organizations die in the process of reproduction, but their substance and essence are maintained in the new firm.

Whatever the method may be, organizations do sometimes engage in the process of reproduction. Organizations reproduce by transforming part of the environment into a copy of themselves. Whether directed by the charter or not, the reproduction process generally requires coordination. Thus, managers must become involved in the process.

Dissemination

Short of creating a new organization, propagation may also occur in the form of disseminating organizational processes, structures, and other memes to the environment. For example, business firms often seek to develop brand loyalty in their customers. To the degree that customers become loyal to a particular brand name, they have accepted important values of the firm that owns the trademark. Another example would be the efforts of the developers of a new video recording system to license their system and influence other manufacturers to accept it as an industry standard. NewVent would like to establish its magnetic flange design as the standard for superior brakes, so that customers will demand it and automobile manufacturers will be compelled to buy it.

Managing such change may require advertising, public relations, and other influence techniques. It may also involve such matters as inventing catchy slogans, designing attractive logos, gathering testimonials from satisfied customers, and lobbying legislators and regulators for decisions that favor our design. Thus, the eighth principle of proactive managed change is

> 8. *Try to influence the environment through reproduction and dissemination to accept and incorporate important values of the organization.*

ORGANIZATIONAL ECOLOGY

Many individuals, groups, organizations, communities, and societies are quite rapacious in their consumption of natural resources such as timber, fish, coal, oil, and copper. To the extent that these resources are irreplaceable or are being depleted more rapidly than they can be replenished, living systems are swiftly reducing the supply of "less critical" resources. The easy shifts of entropy from critical to less-critical resources are disappearing, hastening the time when life will become much more difficult.

Living systems, and organizations in particular, have only a few long-run options. One is to shift to replenishable resources, such as biomass and solar energy, and to consume them only as fast as they can be replaced. Another is to cooperate with other systems in rationing and conserving scarce resources. A third is to compete ferociously in order to attain a place at the top of the food chain.

The choice is ours. The third choice, unbridled competition, may seem easiest. If we choose it, however, we had better recognize that only a few will survive.

DECLINE AND RENEWAL

One major difference between biological and social systems is that the latter are able to renew themselves. Organisms have a life span that is limited, in part, by their own templates. Most organizations, on the other hand, have no such automatic limitations. Nonetheless, without specific interventions designed to renew them, organizations do tend to decline.

The capability for renewal stems from two key characteristics of social systems. First, they are able to change key components much more easily than organisms can. Over a period of time, an organization can replace all of its members, yet still maintain much of its special character as a system. Any corporation that is more than fifty years old has probably already done this. Modern surgical methods are expanding the possibilities of human organ replacement, but it is unlikely that individuals will ever have the renewal capability of organizations.

The second key characteristic is the mutability of memetic templates. When adaptation to environmental change is needed for renewal, it is much easier to modify a corporate charter than to alter genes. Organizations that have survived for hundreds of years, such as certain universities, might be almost unrecognizable to their founders. Yet they have retained their basic character as systems and preserved a core of values. Old universities still hold to the mission with which they were born—preserving, expanding, and disseminating knowledge.

What have changed are some of the methods, structures, and technologies by which that mission is realized. In order to renew themselves in a changing world, universities have modified their rules of governance, sometimes merged with other institutions, learned to finance their activities in new ways, created new departments and colleges, developed new methods of teaching, changed technologies numerous times, and found ways to broaden the base of their appeal.

Business firms have the same opportunities to renew themselves. They do not have to remain in the same niche or stick with the original business ideas that brought them success. They do not have to retain the same personnel or preserve their organizational structure. In fact, if the organization declines, these things will change willy-nilly.

Management is, of course, the key to whether the organization will decline and die or renew itself. The process of renewal must have a vision, a set of new purposes and goals. It must also be coordinated. In short, it requires leadership.

SUMMARY

Change may be unmanaged and may simply happen to the organization; or it may be initiated and managed by the organization. It may be reactive or proactive. It may be initiated for purposes of maintenance, actualization, or propagation. It may be preplanned and directed, at least in part, by the template of the organization; or it may be unforeseen and directed extemporaneously by the decider subsystem. And it may be directed at the process and structure of the organization itself, or at its environment.

Maintenance of the organization requires the following seven types of managed change:

1. *replacing assets lost through entropy,*
2. *adding value sufficient to offset entropic losses,*
3. *correcting process errors,*
4. *adjusting to environmental changes to maintain equilibrium,*
5. *influencing or controlling the environment for greater stability,*
6. *shifting entropic losses from critical to less-critical assets,* and
7. *shifting entropic losses from the system to its environment.*

Actualization of an organization's potential involves four additional kinds of proactive managed change:

1. *adding components and resources in excess of system losses,*
2. *increasing the complexity of the system in accordance with the increasing variety of its environment,*
3. *increasing the complexity of the template and/or decider subsystem in accordance with increasing complexity of the system;* and
4. *recognizing the need for unprogrammed growth and elaboration of the system and coordinating it.*

Reproduction of the organization requires that managers coordinate the process. Dissemination of organizational values and other characteristics calls on managers to exercise influence over the environment. Managers must at times also take a transformational leadership role in order to renew the organization and prevent its decline into oblivion.

NOTES

1. James G. Miller, *Living Systems* (New York: McGraw-Hill, 1978),18.

2. William R. Ashby, *An Introduction to Cybernetics* (New York: Wiley, 1956).

3. R. L. Flood, *Total Quality Management* (Hull, England: The University of Hull, 1990).

4. C. Northcote Parkinson, *Parkinson's Law* (New York: Houghton Mifflin, 1957), 15–27.

Chapter 11

Managing the Future

NewVent has changed. Despite its success and growth in volume of business, the organization is smaller. One whole layer of management has been removed. Manufacturing processes have become highly automated. Machine operators and others on the lowest echelon of the decider subsystem are more involved in planning, scheduling, controlling, and problem solving. Everyone is cross-trained and is expected to wear many hats. Teams of salespeople, engineers, researchers, accountants, and product managers are working closely with customer representatives from the design stage to final assembly and shipping of new products. New products and services are developed much more quickly than before.

The change at UniGlobe has been even more dramatic. Large divisions have been carved up into smaller businesses, so that no unit of the corporation exceeds 400 employees. Except for financial affairs the units are highly autonomous. Twenty-three units employing 7,500 people are managed by a head office of 35 people. Seven layers of management have been reduced to four. Coordination, such as it is, is maintained through an electronic network.

Montero Virtual Realty (MVR) has been less affected by waves of change. It was already a small firm linked to others in an electronic network. But competitive pressures have caused MVR to be constantly looking for new ways to be of service to its customers. In this process, MVR relies heavily on ideas from all employees and from the customers themselves. One innovation has been the formation of interagency teams who "meet" electronically to coordinate intercity sales. Such teams are able to tailor the video presentation of a property to a customer's needs, thereby reducing the need for on-site viewing. Broker's fees are shared.

BRAVE NEW WORLD OF DISORGANIZATION

Tom Peters tells us that in the future our organizations will, of necessity, be more disorganized.[1] They will increasingly resemble professional service organizations—small, fluid, closely tied to the customer, surviving on their ability to respond rapidly. Mass production will yield to "mass customization." Organizations will be flatter, relying heavily on ever-changing project teams rather than on committees and the hierarchy of authority.

Does this mean that organizations will no longer be living systems? Will they simply be loose collections of individuals and short-lived teams?

If we reexamine the essential characteristics of a living system, I think the answer is clearly *no*. The kinds of organizations that Peters describes are still living systems. They possess a centralized decider subsystem that coordinates the diverse activities of the corporation. Indeed, the decider subsystem has been strengthened by modern electronic networks. Some decisions are more centralized than before, whereas others are more decentralized. Peters and Waterman characterized this situation as "simultaneous loose-tight controls."[2]

People continue to be the central components of future organizations. There are more and more automated artifacts helping them, but we are not yet ready to turn everything over to the machines. The template of the organization is still designed by human beings to further collective human interests. The purposes and goals that it specifies are linked to human needs. The template may change more rapidly, or may even be designed to facilitate change, but it has not disappeared.

New Boundaries

One element that is changing, although it still exists, is the boundary subsystem. Boundaries are being drawn more loosely to encompass broader constituencies. "Prosumers"—customers who become actively involved in the process of product design—are becoming part of the organization.[3] Likewise, research and development (R&D) firms are becoming affiliates as organizations farm out more of their R&D work. Furthermore, copying the Japanese style of management, American and European firms are tying themselves closely to single vendors of materials, parts, and subassemblies so that they can exercise greater control over quality and on-time delivery.

The broadening of the boundary poses a problem with respect to the immunity subsubsystem (IS). How is the IS expected to recognize another system as an intruder when, in another context, that same system may be part of the firm? For example, General Motors and Toyota are business rivals who might want to conceal trade secrets from each other, yet they are cooperating in a joint venture to produce automobiles in California. Likewise, customers who are working with NewVent to design better brakes may also be working with NewVent's competitors.

Of course, these boundary problems are not unique to future organizations. Families, the most basic human groups, have always faced them. Many people are members of at least two families, the one that sired them and the one that they formed by marriage. They may be peripheral members of other families as well, as in-laws, uncles and aunts, grandparents, and so forth. The boundary of a family may seem fairly narrow and well defined, but it tends to expand during holidays, birthdays, anniversaries, and times of crisis. Family "secrets" become dispersed through the family grapevine. Claims on inheritance multiply, as do calls for assistance in times of trouble.

Even the boundary of one's own personal system is not that well defined. Many people would want to include within their personal boundary both the clothes they wear and the car they drive. "Clothes make the man," so to speak. For women who are pregnant, a decision about abortion involves the question of whether the fetus is part of themselves or a separate living entity.

Living systems must have a boundary *somewhere*, but its shape may change depending on context. If the boundaries of modern organizations seem amorphous, it is only a matter of degree. All boundaries are somewhat indeterminate.

The key to defining the boundary of an organization at any given moment lies in observing what the organization is able to keep out when it wants to. A customer may be allowed into team meetings on product design, but not into the boardroom. Competitors may share in profits from a joint venture, but not in each other's profits as a whole. Hourly paid employees may enter the premises to work but may be excluded from decision making or profit sharing.

New Organizational Forms and Niches

Advances in technology have enabled organizations to invade new environmental niches, such as aquaculture and biogenetics. Improved communications technology has also led to the development of new forms of organization. These novel forms are sometimes the result of technological innovation that enables organizations to carry out their processes in new ways. In other cases, they are the result of experimentation in how to succeed in new environments.

An early example of an advance in communications technology that spawned a novel organizational form to tackle a new niche was the invention of the telegraph and the subsequent growth of railroads. Until the development of the telegraph, railroads were local operations limited to a length of a few miles. The telegraph made it possible for railroads to maintain rapid internal information flow at a distance. Seeing the potential of offering rapid, scheduled transport services over long distances, entrepreneurs created a new form of geographically dispersed, telegraph-linked organizations to exploit that niche.

The development of almost instantaneous global communications by means of satellites has greatly spurred the growth of multinational organizations. Multinational business firms are now able to compete more effectively because their natural advantages, such as economies of scale and ability to shift resources where they can be most effective, are no longer impeded by slow and inadequate information flow.

Already multinational corporations are yielding to a new form of *multidomestic firm* in which each unit customizes its output for the local market.[4] New information technology permits a worldwide organization to combine the advantages of economies of scale and core production technologies with local knowledge of market needs and preferences.

Another new form that is now taking hold is the *teleorganization*. It consists of people and departments that may never see each other face to face, but who maintain contact entirely through electronic means. Computer networks, conference calls, and FAXes take the place of meetings and conversations. The richness of the electronic means has become sufficient to allow development of personal relationships, loyalty, and a distinct organizational culture even without personal contact.

A teleorganization can offer services in a wide variety of locations close to the customers, while still maintaining some facets of central control and standardization. The members can operate from their own homes or at satellite offices without having to waste hours commuting to and from work. And, of course, the teleorganization can function efficiently in a multinational environment.

Another new form is the *micro-organization*. In many industries, we are seeing very small firms springing up and being able to compete with the giants, because the technology for performing very complex tasks is being simplified. For example, microbreweries are now vying very successfully with the brewers of nationwide brands of beer. Brewing technology has been packaged into small, efficient plants that require few operators and can make a very good product.

Another example is the proliferation of small firms producing and marketing personal computers. Because the heart of these computers has been consolidated on a few widely available chips, what once required a very complex assembly process has now been reduced to a task that can be performed in a basement workshop.

Multidomestic firms, micro-organizations, teleorganizations, and other new forms have yet to receive much attention from organization theorists. What we know about organizational structure has mainly been derived from the study of large national corporations like General Motors and AT&T and, more recently, from analysis of multinationals. We need to begin to look at other alternatives.

Living systems theory offers an excellent framework for examining new forms and assessing their viability. Looking at teleorganizations, for instance, the theory causes us to focus on the adequacy of the boundary, the decider subsystem, and the channel and net subsystem. Can such a widely dispersed organization defend itself from unwanted intrusions and retain needed resources? Does current electronic technology really offer an adequate substitute for personal contact and direct dialogue when making important decisions? Would videophones improve the richness of communications and the cohesiveness of the organization, or would they simply introduce unnecessary extra costs? Does reliance on electronic communications increase the need for standard policies and procedures (i.e., a more elaborate template), or is it better to decentralize operations and rely more on the training and loyalty of the dispersed work force? Should the employees at least get together for training or an annual meeting? We do not yet have answers for these questions, but living systems theory points the way toward the answers we need as we try new forms of organization and explore new environmental niches.

ORGANIZATION WITHIN DISORGANIZATION

From a living systems point of view, "disorganization" is an inaccurate term for what is happening to business firms and, to a lesser extent, government bureaus. In some respects, our organizations are more tightly linked than ever before. Communications are faster and fuller, enabling improved interchange of ideas. Indeed that is why, as Peters says, the success of organizations is increasingly based on knowledge rather than production capability.[5] Better communication capabilities allow greater accountability. Accountability provides discipline to the organization in spite of its looser, more flexible structure.[6]

What seems to be happening to organizations is that, in response to a rapidly changing, highly competitive environment, they are becoming less structured and more process centered. You may recall that structure is simply a snapshot of the arrangement of a system's components and subsystems at a moment in time. If we use a faster shutter speed, we will still find structure underlying a fast-changing organization's processes. But structure has become relatively unimportant. What counts today is that processes are flexible and adaptive, yet still responsive to the organization's purposes and goals.

"Organization" is not dead, but organizations that try to maintain the old style of rigid structure and tight bureaucratic control may be dying. It is not that such organizations are an inherently flawed form of life. In their time they were very successful. But they are dinosaurs and this is not the era of dinosaurs. Other forms of organizational life have emerged that are better adapted to today's environment.

Adaptation is a key element of life. In Chapter 10, however, we noted several levels of adaptability. In the short term, organizations must react to change in order to maintain their structure and processes. Yet that alone is not enough. Organizations must also grow and develop in accordance with the mandate of their own abilities. Beyond that, they must learn and adapt to a changing environment. It is this last form of adaptation that appears to have become preeminent in today's business world.

One caveat should be given. Change should not be pursued for its own sake. It is still necessary to maintain certain steady states, even in the most adaptive organization. If the structure of the organization is fluid, for instance, then perhaps the members themselves become more important as an element of stability. Something about the organization must remain constant as it changes, or else the system *does* disappear.

THE LIVING FUTURE

It is an exciting time for living organizations. Volcanoes of technology are erupting. Faster communications and transport are pushing the continents closer together. Organizational species that have been protected by isolation and legislation are now being subjected to attack by new predators. Their adaptability will be tested. If they do not learn new defenses, they may not survive.

Managers are key elements in the adaptability of organizations. They hold the levers of change in their hands. It is tempting for managers to think that they must personally slay the dragons, quell the volcanoes, and reorganize the system. Yet they should not think that they must do it alone. In fact, it has been proven time after time that lasting change in an organization is facilitated by involvement of all its members. This is especially true if the organization is regarded as an independent entity, rather than a puppet or a possession.

The manager's real task is to organize and coordinate the efforts of the entire organization in the direction of continuous improvement. Here we mean more than improvement of the production process; the goal of continuous improvement should be applied to the organization as a whole. The organization should be striving to become better adapted to its environment and more effective in meeting its objectives and satisfying its constituencies.

Living systems theory is a diagnostic tool that can aid managers in their task of leading the organization toward continuous improvement. Keep in mind, however, that the theory itself is in the process of development. Modify it and expand it as you see fit. It is an instrument for seeing more clearly, not a straitjacket.

NOTES

1. Tom Peters, *Liberation Management: Necessary Disorganization for the Nanosecond Nineties* (New York: Knopf, 1992).

2. Thomas J. Peters and Robert H. Waterman, Jr., *In Search of Excellence: Lessons from America's Best-Run Companies* (New York: Harper & Row, 1982).

3. Alvin Toffler, *The Third Wave* (New York: Morrow, 1980).

4. Peters, *Liberation Management*, 46.

5. Ibid., 21.

6. Ibid., 26.

Glossary

Adjustment processes: subsystem processes that counteract entropy and environmental stresses in order to maintain steady states in a living system. *Examples:* perspiring to maintain constant body temperature, adjusting production schedules to maintain a steady flow of products.

Agreed system: a system of interaction that results from negotiation; may be a living system whose template is the agreement between other systems. *Examples:* a joint venture, a trading partnership.

Artifact: a part of a living system that is made by plants, animals, or man; an artificial inclusion in a system. *Examples:* machinery, clothing, eyeglasses, dental fillings.

Association: the perceived likelihood that an act will lead to a given outcome or that the outcome will result in a particular reward. *Examples:* the expectancy that a certain job can be completed in two hours is high; the likelihood that completion of the job will lead to promotion is perceived as low.

Associator: the critical subsystem that forms lasting associations among items of information. *Examples:* associating a word with an object or action, linking a bill of sale with the proper account.

Boundary: the critical subsystem that surrounds and protects components of a living system, acts as a barrier to free movement of matter-energy and information in and out of the system, and filters inputs and outputs by allowing some but not others to pass. *Examples:* the skin and clothing of a person; the buildings, grounds, gates, docks, receptionists, and interviewers of a corporation.

Channel and net: the critical subsystem that carries information-bearing markers around the system. *Examples:* the human nervous system, a computer network or intercom system.

Component: a concrete, identifiable structural unit of a living system; also called *part* or *member*; may be a living system in its own right. *Examples:* a machine, employee, or department in an organization.

Conflict: a strain that occurs when a system is required to respond simultaneously to two or more commands that are incompatible. *Example:* a manager is in conflict when required to carry out an order against his better judgment.

Conflict management: the process of maintaining sufficient conflict for motivation while keeping it from interfering with necessary cooperation.

Conflict resolution: the process of reducing conflict to a minimum or eliminating it.

Converter: the critical subsystem that changes certain inputs into forms that are more useful for other processes of the system. *Examples:* teeth grinding food into a more digestible form, a furnace that converts fuel into heat.

Cooperation: the process of two or more systems working together toward a common goal for mutual benefit. *Example:* two firms cooperating to obtain a contract that neither of them could fulfill alone.

Decider: the critical subsystem that makes choices based on the system's hierarchy of values and implements those choices. *Examples:* the brain and "nervous system" of mammals, the hierarchy of executives, managers, supervisors, and operatives in an organization.

Decoder: the critical subsystem that alters the code of information input into a private code used by the system. *Examples:* perception of symbolic language, translation from one language to another, writing orders using the special numbers and terminology of the firm.

Distress: a pathological condition of a system, resulting from the inability of the system to relieve a strain. *Example:* an employee suffers distress because he or she cannot cope with his or her workload.

Distributor: the critical subsystem that carries matter and energy around the system to each component. *Examples:* the blood stream, conveyor belts and fork lifts.

Dyad: a system composed of two interacting living systems; may also be a living system itself. *Examples:* employer and employee, husband and wife.

Efficiency: the ratio of the worth of outputs to the cost of producing them. *Example:* if something can be sold for $30 and the cost of producing it is $20, the efficiency of the system in this case is 30/20 or 150 percent.

Emergent: a characteristic manifested in higher level systems but not in lower level systems. *Example:* symbolic representation and speech emerging at the level of higher organisms.

Encoder: the critical subsystem that alters the code of information from the system's private code into one that can be interpreted by other systems. *Examples:* converting concepts and images into words, translating the firm's private jargon into standard English.

Entropy: the universal tendency toward disorder or randomness; inevitable loss of available energy. *Example:* the dissipation of heat from a cup of coffee standing at room temperature.

Extruder: the critical subsystem that moves products and wastes across the boundary into the environment. *Examples:* the body parts and artifacts that eliminate human waste, the shipping and sanitation departments of a corporation.

Force of motivation: the strength of push or pull toward a particular act; the sum of the products of valences and associations linked to the prospective outcomes of that act. *Example:* a firm expectancy (association) of increased pay (valence) creates a strong force toward work.

Goal: a system's preference for something external to the system, such as a relationship with another system; an external target. *Examples:* a sales target of $1 million per month, a 30 percent market share, 50 new members.

Homeostasis: the tendency of system variables to return to their original values when disturbed. *Example:* when the amount of an item in inventory reaches the reorder point, the system purchases or produces more of the item to replenish the inventory.

Immunity subsubsystem (IS): a subsystem of the boundary that provides reactive defenses against various external threats and internal disruptions. *Examples:* a fire brigade and automatic sprinkler system, supervision of employee behavior.

Inclusion: a part of the environment that crosses the boundary of a system and becomes surrounded by the system, but does not become part of the system. *Example:* a salesperson who enters the premises of a customer.

Ingestor: the critical subsystem that brings matter and energy across the boundary into the system. *Examples:* mouth and nose, receiving department, electric mains.

Input transducer: the critical subsystem of sensors that bring markers bearing information into the system, changing them into other forms suitable for transmission within the system. *Examples:* eyes and ears, in organizations, combined with artifacts such as telephones, FAX machines.

Interface: the common boundary of two systems or a system and its environment. *Examples:* a meeting between representatives of two organizations, the surface of the skin.

Internal transducer: the critical subsystem of sensors that receive information-bearing markers from other subsystems or components of the system and change them into forms suitable for transmission within the system. *Examples:* pain receptors, smoke detectors, internal audits.

Leadership: Purposeful assumption of some or all of the processes of the top echelon of the decider subsystem for a social system. *Examples:* CEO of a corporation, president or prime minister of a nation.

Marker: an observable bundle, unit, or change in matter-energy, the patterning of which carries information. *Examples:* the bundles of ink that form the letters on this page, the changes in air pressure (i.e., waves) that carry speech to your ears.

Meaning: the significance of information to a system that processes it; a change in that system's processes. *Examples:* a person hears the word "dinner" and starts to move toward the dinner table, an order clerk reads an order and begins to gather the materials to fill it.

Meme: an idea or set of ideas that has the capability of generating systems to reproduce it, or inducing existing systems to reproduce it. *Examples:* a fad or fashion, a play, a charter for a sorority, a chemical formula.

Memetic template: the set of memes that supply instructions for growing and maintaining a social system. *Examples:* group norms, a corporate charter, franchise agreement, city charter, constitution.

Memory: the critical subsystem that stores information-bearing markers, maintains them, and retrieves them. *Examples:* cramming for a test and recalling the information for an exam, using artifacts such as libraries and computer disks.

Motor: the critical subsystem that moves the system or components of it in relation to its environment, or moves parts of the environment in relation to each other. *Examples:* our limbs, the company motor pool.

Multidomestic firm: a multinational firm in which each unit customizes its output for the local market. *Example:* ABB (Asea Brown Boveri).

Negentropy: the opposite of entropy; maintenance of order. *Example:* living systems strive to maintain order within themselves and their environment.

Negotiation: a process of communication between living systems with the goal of reaching agreement about certain joint or reciprocal acts. *Example:* bargaining between a firm and a vendor for a purchasing contract.

Node: an intersection of information channels that introduces no deliberate change in signals that pass through it. *Examples:* a telephone switching station, a messenger.

Open system: a system that receives inputs from its environment, transforms them, and expels products or wastes. *Examples:* automobiles, plants, dogs.

Output transducer: the critical subsystem that changes the system's markers into forms suitable for transmission outside of the system, and transmits them. *Examples:* putting thoughts into spoken words, sending computer data through a modem.

Power: possession or control of excess resources that are valued positively or negatively by another system. *Example:* a manager who controls opportunities for promotion has power over those who desire a better job.

Purpose: a specific preferred steady-state value for a system variable. *Examples:* a person's body has a purpose of maintaining a constant body temperature, represented by a reading of $98.6°$ F on an oral thermometer, an organization sets a purpose of maintaining cash reserves of $100,000.

Reproducer: the critical subsystem that transmits information that becomes the template of a new system similar to the original, and assembles matter-energy to compose the new system. *Examples:* the set of male and female sexual organs in mammals, the franchising subsystem of a retail chain.

Resource: anything that is capable of fulfilling a need. *Examples:* air for air-breathing animals, raw materials for a manufacturing firm.

Social power: power over people or other social systems. See *Power.*

Social system: a living system above the organism level; an association of organisms. *Examples:* groups, organizations, communities, societies, the United Nations.

Stakeholder: a constituency; for a firm, other systems that hold an interest in the success of the firm. *Examples:* stockholders, employees, customers, suppliers, creditors, the community, government agencies.

Strain: deviation of a system variable beyond its range of stability; a lack or excess of a resource. *Examples:* an influx of new orders creates a strain on production scheduling, late payments cause a strain on cash flow.

Stress: an input or output that forces one or more system variables beyond their range of stability; not to be confused with *distress. Example:* a heavy influx of orders overloads the production subsystem.

Subsystem: the collection of structures in a living system that carry out a particular process. *Examples:* the collection of nerves and brain tissue that supply the decider process for an organism, the buildings that carry out the supporter process for a business firm.

Supporter: the critical subsystem that maintains a proper spatial relationship among components of the system. *Examples:* the human skeleton and muscles, the walls, partitions, and floors of the building(s) housing an organization.

Suprasystem: for any living system, the next higher system of which it is a component or subsystem. *Examples:* the organ of which a cell is a part, the family of a person, the community in which a firm does business.

Teleorganization: an organization of people and departments who maintain contact entirely through electronic means. *Examples:* a nationwide realty network, an international news organization.

Template: a set of instructions for developing and maintaining the basic structure and processes of a living system; it exists at the origin of the system. *Examples:* the genetic material in any organism, in part, a charter or business plan for an organization.

Timer: the critical subsystem that transmits signals of time and pace to the decider of the system and the deciders of its components. *Examples:* the signals that regulate the heartbeat and the menstrual cycle, punchclocks, lunch whistles, and calendars in a factory.

Totipotential: capable of carrying out all of the critical processes that are necessary for life. A system that must rely on other systems for some of these processes is called *partipotential. Example:* a healthy adult human being is totipotential, an infant is partipotential.

Transformational leadership: leadership that appeals to the higher interests of the membership and inspires them with a new vision of what the organization can be. *Example:* Lee Iacocca rallying Chrysler Corp. from the brink of bankruptcy.

Usefulness: the characteristic of a resource or product that gives it worth in the eyes of a living system. *Example:* a useful product can be sold for more money than it cost to produce and sell it.

Valence: the estimated worth of prospective outcomes of an act. *Examples:* the promotion that might result from making a big sale has high positive valence, the effort required to make the sale has a negative valence.

Selected Bibliography

Argyris, Chris, and D. A. Schon. *Organizational Learning: A Theory of Action Perspective*. Reading, MA: Addison-Wesley, 1978.

Bass, Bernard M. *Leadership and Performance Beyond Expectations*. New York: Free Press, 1985.

Bennis, Warren G., and Burt Nanus. *Leaders: The Strategies for Taking Charge*. New York: Harper & Row, 1985.

Cavaleri, Steven, and Krzysztof Obloj. *Management Systems: A Global Perspective*. Belmont, CA: Wadsworth, 1993.

Crosby, Philip B. *Quality without Tears*. New York: McGraw-Hill, 1984.

Daft, Richard L., and Karl E. Weick. "Toward a model of organizations as interpretation systems." *Academy of Management Review* 9 (1984): 284–95.

Dawkins, Richard. *The Selfish Gene*. New York: Oxford University Press, 1976.

Deming, W. Edwards. *Out of the Crisis*. Cambridge, MA: MIT Center for Advanced Engineering Study, 1982.

Drexler, K. Eric. *Engines of Creation: The Coming Era of Nanotechnology*. New York: Doubleday, 1986.

Feigenbaum, A. V. *Total Quality Control*. New York: McGraw-Hill, 1983.

Fisher, Roger, and William Ury. *Getting to Yes: Negotiating Agreement without Giving In*, 2d ed. New York: Penguin, 1991.

Flood, Robert L. *Total Quality Management*. Hull, England: The University of Hull, 1990.

Goldratt, Eliyahu M., and Jeff Cox. *The Goal: A Process of Ongoing Improvement*, 2d ed. Croton-on-Hudson, NY: North River, 1992.

Gray, Barbara. *Collaborating: Finding Common Ground for Multiparty Problems*. San Francisco: Jossey-Bass, 1989.

Jaros, Gyorgy G., and Anacreon Cloete. "Biomatrix: The web of life." *World Futures* 23 (1987): 203–24.

Juran, J. M. *Juran on Planning for Quality.* New York: Free Press, 1988.

———. *Juran on Leadership for Quality: An Executive Handbook.* New York: Free Press, 1989.

Kennedy, Paul. *The Rise and Fall of the Great Powers.* New York: Random House, 1987.

Lawler, Edward E., III. *The Ultimate Advantage: Creating the High-Involvement Organization.* San Francisco: Jossey-Bass, 1992.

Lax, David A., and James K. Sebenius. *The Manager as Negotiator: Bargaining for Cooperation and Competitive Gain.* New York: Free Press, 1986.

Merker, Stephen L. "A living systems process analysis of an urban hospital." *Behavioral Science* 32 (1987): 304–14.

Miller, James G. *Living Systems.* New York: McGraw-Hill, 1978.

Miller, James G., and Jessie L. Miller. "A living systems analysis of organizational pathology." *Behavioral Science* 36 (1991): 239–52.

Miller, Jessie L. "The timer." *Behavioral Science* 35 (1990): 164–96.

Miller, Jessie L., and James G. Miller. "Greater than the sum of its parts." *Behavioral Science* 37 (1992): 1–38.

Mitroff, Ian I. *Stakeholders of the Organizational Mind.* San Francisco: Jossey-Bass, 1983.

Morgan, Gareth. *Images of Organization.* Newbury Park, CA: Sage, 1986.

Ott, J. Steven. *The Organizational Culture Perspective.* Chicago: Dorsey Press, 1989.

Pauchant, Thierry C., and Ian I. Mitroff. *Transforming the Crisis-Prone Organization: Preventing Individual, Organizational, and Environmental Tragedies.* San Francisco: Jossey-Bass, 1992.

Peters, Thomas J., and Robert H. Waterman, Jr. *In Search of Excellence: Lessons from America's Best-Run Companies.* New York: Harper & Row, 1982.

Peters, Tom. *Liberation Management: Necessary Disorganization for the Nanosecond Nineties.* New York: Knopf, 1992.

Rahim, M. Afzalur. *Managing Conflict: An Interdisciplinary Approach.* Westport, CT: Praeger, 1989.

Sathe, Vijay. "Implications of corporate culture: A manager's guide to action." *Organizational Dynamics* 12, no. 2 (1983): 5–23.

Schein, Edgar H. *Organizational Culture and Leadership: A Dynamic View.* San Francisco: Jossey-Bass, 1991.

Swanson, G. A., and Hugh L. Marsh. *Internal Auditing Theory—A Systems View.* Westport, CT: Quorum Books, 1991.

Swanson, G. A., and James G. Miller. *Measurement and Interpretation in Accounting: A Living Systems Theory Approach.* Westport, CT: Quorum Books, 1989.

Tichy, Noel, and Mary Anne Devanna. *Transformational Leadership.* New York: Wiley, 1986.

Toffler, Alvin. *The Third Wave.* New York: Morrow, 1980.

———. *The Adaptive Corporation.* New York: McGraw-Hill, 1985.

———. *Powershift: Knowledge, Wealth, and Violence at the Edge of the 21st Century.* New York: Bantam, 1990.

Tracy, Lane. "Toward an improved need theory: In response to legitimate criticism." *Behavioral Science* 31 (1986): 205–18.

———. *The Living Organization: Systems of Behavior.* Westport, CT: Praeger, 1989.

———. "Immunity and error correction: System design for organizational defense." *Systems Practice* 6 (1993): 259–74.

Ury, William. *Getting Past No: Negotiating with Difficult People.* New York: Bantam, 1991.

Vroom, Victor H., and Arthur G. Jago. *The New Leadership: Managing Participation in Organizations.* Englewood Cliffs, NJ: Prentice Hall, 1988.

Walton, Mary. *The Deming Management Method.* New York: Perigee, 1986.

———. *Deming Management at Work.* New York: G. P. Putnam's Sons, 1990.

Index

abuse, drug and alcohol, 29, 132–33
acquired immune deficiency syndrome
(AIDS), 144
acts: choice of, 49–50; joint or reciprocal, 126–27, 139
actualization: change for, 176–80; management for, 184
adaptation, organizational, 98
adjudication, conflict management
and, 126
adjustment processes, 32, 87, 142, 174
agreed system, 138–41; behavior of,
139; components of, 140; template
of, 140; temporary, 140; types of,
139–41
agreement: implementation of, 128–29,
138; reaching, 126–30; as template
for new system, 138
appeasement, conflict management
and, 126
Apple Computer, 10
arbitration, conflict management and,
126
artifact, 7, 34, 38, 71, 186; of an organization, 7
aspirations, customer satisfaction and,
114–15

assets: critical, 175–76; critical, substitutes for, 176, 182; replacement of,
173, 176; worth of, 66
association between act and outcome,
51; alteration of, 53, 57
associator process, 36–37; dispersal of,
36, 88–89
associator subsystem, 88–89; artifacts
of, 88–89
AT&T (American Telephone and Telegraph), 189
authority: centralization of, 47; clarifying lines of, 32; conflict management and, 125–26, 138; hierarchy of,
186
automation, cost reduction through, 66
avoidance: conflict management and,
126, 138; and terms of exchange,
138

bargaining, levels of, 138–39
behavior: of agreed system, 139; baseline of, 132–33; choice of, 49; consistency of, 45; continuation of
current, 51–53; decider–directed,
48; direction of, 41–42, 45, 52;
innate, 45; instinctive, 43–48; inten-

living systems process analysis, 58
living systems theory, 14–15; and conflict, 133, 163, 168; as a diagnostic
tool, 191; and immunity, 141; and
leadership, 158, 168; and motivation, 42–43; and negotiation, 127;
and new organizational forms, 189;
and planning a new organization,
19, 25, 39
Locke, Edwin A., 49
loyalty: brand, 181; conflict of, 124;
divided, of leaders, 157, 160, 162,
165–66; organizational, 72

Machiavellianism, 167
management: of change, 171–79; of
production, 105; of resources, 79–80
manager, 1–3; and motivation, 50, 52–
54, 56–59; need for a, 66; and organizational adaptability, 190; and
power, 79, 81; reproductive role of a,
107; roles of a, 3–4, 15, 110
markers, 33–36, 62, 65, 86–90; electronic, 65; and media, 34
market, estimating the, 21–22
matter: consumption of, 62–63, 172;
inputs of, 62–63; transformation of,
63
matter-energy processes, 13, 37–39; and
quality, 114
matter-energy subsystems, 105–14;
pathologies of, 117–18. *See also specific subsystems*
maturity, organizational, 30
media of communication, 99–100;
selecting, 95
membership, indicators of, 143
memes, 7, 24, 181
memory process, 36–37, 73; dispersal
of, 89; stages of, 89
memory subsystem, 71–72, 74, 89; artifacts of, 89; role of members in, 89
merger: of decider subsystems, 127; as
means of reproduction, 181; of systems, 11, 68, 138
micro-organization, 188–89

Miller, James G., 7, 12, 14, 31, 84, 122,
142
mission of the firm, 42
model: of communication between
systems, 99; of decider-directed
motivation, 49–50; of dyadic
negotiation, 129–30; homeostatic,
49; of motivational interaction,
54–55; of template-directed motivation, 48
money: accessibility of, 65; as a carrier
of resources, 65–66; as a critical
resource, 22, 65–66; as a facilitator
of exchange, 70, 81; as information,
33; storability of, 65
Morgan, Gareth, 17 n.1
motivation, 15; decider-directed, 49–53;
differences in, 41–43; of employees,
42; force of, 50; human, 42; of a
manager, 42; of an organization, 42–
43, 56; processes of, 41–53; reciprocal, 54; sources of, 46; template-
directed, 43–49
motivational interaction, 53–56
motives, influences on, 42
motor process, 38–39; dispersal of, 112
motor subsystem, 111–12; member
roles in, 112
Murray, Henry A., 44

nation, 6–10. *See also* society
need fulfillment, 42, 46, 49–52
needs, 1–2, 15, 42, 45–50; active, 46;
competing, 49; hierarchy of, 50;
human, 45–46, 186; importance of,
50; intensity of, 50; of an organization, 46, 56, 62; and power, 76; stim-
ulation of, 52, 57
need theory, 49, 54
negentropy, steady state of, 172; and
maintenance of usefulness, 172
negotiation, 26, 126–32; and agreed
systems, 139–41; collaborative, 131–
32; communication and, 126, 128–
29; goals of, 139–41; models of, 128–
31; between organizations, 138; preparedness in, 132, and the repro-

of, 26, 40; elaboration of, 178; fray-out, 14–15. *See also names of specific processes*

producer process, 38, 75; and converter process, 108, 110; dispersal of the, 38, 110; selling as a, 109

producer subsystem, 108–10; artifacts of, 110; buffering of, 109; member roles in, 109–10; pathologies of, 117

production, 109; maintaining a steady flow of, 174; to order, 105

products, 62–63; and services, 105; value of, 111

profit: declining, 145; as a goal, 31, 33, 43, 56, 58, 97, 114, 116

profitability, 138, 173

protoplasm, 6, 14

purposes, 31, 42, 45, 49, 59, 158; alignment of, between levels, 160; changing, 167; degree of attainment of, 66; hierarchy of, 49; organizational, 4, 14, 31, 59, 116; sources of, 42, 59

purpose value, deviation from, 48

quality: control over, 186; and customer satisfaction, 114–15

quality circles, 98

Raven, Bertram, 77

reflex, 44–45; unconditioned, 44

reinforcement theory, 44, 49, 51, 54

relationship: dyadic, 67–68; environmental, 135–36; exchange, 68–71, 136–37; external, 68

renewal, organizational, 166, 182–83

reproducer process, 26–28, 181; and assistance, 28

reproducer subsystem, 85, 106–7; and negotiation, 139

reproduction: organizational, 107, 181, 184; sexual, 6, 9–10, 181–82

resources, 4, 8, 21, 62; acquisition of, 26, 62, 136; availability of, 62; carrier of, 64–65; competition for, 5; consumption of natural, 182; control over, 11; deficiency of, in environment, 37; excess of, 45, 76–80; exchange of,

136; expenditure of, 49; flow of, 1, 8, 62, 68–70, 172; forms of, 62–66; human, 64–65; informational, 26; lack of, 45, 56; matter-energy, 26, 62–63; nonrenewable, 75, 182; renewable, 64, 75, 182; required, 42; storage of, 71–76; substitution of, 62, 75, 137

response, conditioned, 44

responsibilities: compartmentalization of, 162–64; division of, 165

risk, management of, 73–76

role: conflict in, 124–25; of physician, 3–4; sender of, 124; of steward, 3–4

Sebenius, James K., 127

selectivity, 2; of boundary subsystem, 142

self, distinguishing from other, 143

service (business), 22

Skinner, B. F., 44

social learning theory, 49

social power, 76–79; bases of, 77; countervailing, 81; effectiveness of, 77–78, 80–81; limits of, 78; net, 79; and perception, 76–78, 80–81; two-way, 79

social system, 6–12, 14; capability for renewal of, 182; evolution of, 146; and resource exchange, 81; and social power, 76

society, 9, 11, 182. *See also* nation

spirit, entrepreneurial, 20

stability, range of: and need, 45–46, 48; and stress, 132

stakeholders, 116–17, 155–56; values of, 116

steady state: maintenance of, 172, 190; preferred, 45

storage: cost of, 66, 110; of resources, 71–76

storage capacity, 71–72, 137; and efficiency, 72–73; expansion of, 71–74; innate, 72–73; limits to, 74–76; optimal, 74–75; organizational, 71, 74–75

storage process, 38, 63; dispersal of, 110; stages of, 38, 110

vaccination, 148–49
valence of prospective outcome, 50–53
values, 4, 14–15, 66; and conflict, 124, 162–63; core of, 183; hierarchy of, 122–23, 125; homogenization of, 164–65, 169; of negotiating parties, 129; organizational, 28–29, 115, 161, 163–65; personal, 164–65; pluralism of, 165, 168; propagation of, 181; of workers, 115
venture, joint, 11, 20, 26, 76, 139–41, 181,187

Vroom, Victor H., 49

waste, 37, 46, 62–63, 111
Waterman, Robert H., Jr., 59, 186
World Court, 141
worth, 3; added, 173; changing, 115; claiming, 127; creating, 127, 129; and efficiency, 66, 80, 115; of information, 63–64; in the marketplace, 115; and money, 65; of output, 50–52, 66, 115; and power, 76–77; of resources consumed, 66

About the Author

LANE TRACY is Professor of Management at the College of Business Administration, Ohio University, and formerly editor-in-chief of the *Mid-American Journal of Business*. A member of many professional organizations and contributor of articles on living systems theory, labor-management cooperation, and other topics, he is the author of several scholarly and professional books, among them *The Living Organization: Systems of Behavior* (Praeger, 1989).

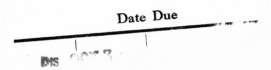